Christmas in July?

Brookings Occasional Papers

Christmas in July?

The Political Economy of
German Unification Reconsidered

ULLRICH HEILEMANN AND REIMUT JOCHIMSEN

THE BROOKINGS INSTITUTION

Washington, D.C.

Brookings Occasional Papers

THE BROOKINGS INSTITUTION is a private nonprofit organization devoted to research, education, and publication on important issues of domestic and foreign policy. Its principal purpose is to bring knowledge to bear on the major policy problems facing the American people.

On occasion Brookings staff members produce research papers that warrant immediate circulation as contributions to the public debate on current issues of national importance. Because of the speed of their production, these Occasional Papers are not subjected to all of the formal review procedures established for the Institution's research publications, and they may be revised at a later date. As in all Brookings publications, the judgments, conclusions, and recommendations presented in the Papers are solely those of the authors and should not be attributed to the trustees, officers, or other staff members of the Institution.

Acknowledgements

This paper is an expanded and updated version of the authors' presentations at a Brookings Institution workshop, "The New Germany and the New Europe," September 8–11, 1991, in Rottach-Egern, Germany. The authors benefited greatly from the discussion there. Particular thanks go to Werner Meißner, Wolfgang Reinicke, and John Steinbruner. James Schneider edited the manuscript, Susanne Lane prepared it for typesetting, and Susan Woollen typeset it.

People are said to be eager to celebrate anniversaries because their collective memory is so short-lived. For Germans, the dizzying pace of change in east Germany since the establishment of the Monetary, Economic, and Social Union (MESU) between the German Democratic Republic and the Federal Republic of Germany on July 1, 1990, and the signing of the Unification Treaty on October 3, 1990, makes this forgetfulness easy to understand. The second anniversary of unification can thus serve to revive collective German memory.[1] But it can also serve a more important purpose.

It is important to remember that political leaders, academics, and business people grossly underestimated the difficulty of reconstructing the east German economy. The underestimation is now universally acknowledged, and despite the recrimination it has sometimes inspired, the situation is understandable. But even judging by more realistic expectations, the progress made since 1990, despite the many mistakes and oversights, has been remarkable. Nevertheless, the initial miscalculation has not been fully overcome, and the basic question regarding the east German economy has not been adequately addressed: Can gradual adjustments vitalize it or is a complete overhaul, reaching to the foundations of the economy and society, necessary?

There are some encouraging signs in east Germany, in part because west German and European Community commitments of time and money substantially exceeded commitments envisioned at the outset of unification. The immense sums already spent, however, have only hinted at the magnitude of the ultimate requirement. Nor have the timing of those efforts and their workability been realistically estimated. There is, for example, a common presumption that east German and west German standards of living must be equalized reasonably soon. That is clearly desirable, but its feasibility remains a serious question.

Though it is still too early to pass final judgment on the speed, methods, or results of east Germany's reconstruction, including the effectiveness of the various policies executed or under way, it is not too early to identify an emerging presumption. It now appears that a

1

complete reorientation of the society and the economy of the former GDR is unavoidable. Although historically part of one Germany, for forty years the FRG and the GDR diverged in many basic ways. A reorientation is requiring more than the twelve to fifteen months characteristic of the slowdown and revival of the business cycle in Western industrialized economies, the length of time that seems to have been assumed by many observers in 1990. In addition, though massive public expenditure programs and investment incentives are under way, their multiplier effects are diminished by east Germany's high propensity to import from west Germany and the inability of east German producers to compete. Finally, of greatest concern to the FRG's neighbors is that unification's political demands and the consequences of its economic, fiscal, and monetary policies must be expected to govern its actions for many years to come. Although Eastern and Western Europe and other parts of the world once anticipated a strengthened German commitment of resources, Germany will have to plead an inadequate budget. Given the magnitude of the demands of unification, further resources will be difficult to find.

The following analysis of German unification—its driving and retarding forces and their direction and size—is an initial effort to address these matters. It reviews the framework of unification, the events, and the reactions. Yet it has to be selective. The policy and performance of the Treuhandanstalt, the east German privatization agency, can only be outlined. The fiscal and monetary policies of the Länder (states) and the communities in east Germany have been mostly ignored. As for monetary policy and its consequences for interest and exchange rates, though it is more important for east Germany than often realized, rates will respond mainly to the expansionary west German fiscal policy (as described by the Mundell-Fleming model) and its stability goals.

The paper begins by identifying the difficulties in forecasting east Germany's short- and longer-term development prospects. The second section evaluates the economic situation since July 1, 1990, and takes stock of the fundamental changes that the Monetary, Economic, and Social Union and the political unification of October 1990 imposed on east Germany's economy. The third section distinguishes the elements unique to the current situation and other elements with precedents or parallels in the past. The fourth section examines the fiscal and financial implications of unification, and the fifth focuses on the difficulties of improving east Germany's poor productivity and high unemploy-

2

ment. To show the magnitude of the tasks and to suggest ways of solving them, the sixth section outlines the structural readjustment that took place in North Rhine–Westphalia in the past thirty years in response to a severe economic downturn. The seventh section discusses the future relationship between the federal government and the Länder (the German states) and the new Germany's role in the new Europe. The eighth section considers the role economists played inside and outside the administration during the planning and implementation of economic unification. The final section offers observations on current policies and trends set in motion by unification. A chronology of the main economic and political events and the resulting policies follows in the appendix.

East Germany's Catch-up: Guessing Policies and Parameters

For now, forecasts of east Germany's economic future have to be based almost entirely on assumptions about the size of its exports and the investment, government transfers, and subsidies it will receive. Reactions to these will for some time be difficult to quantify. Although this paper does not evaluate current forecasts for the FRG's growth as a whole, tables 1 and 2 give an overview of short-term development in east and west Germany as seen from the vantage point of fall 1992. The economic indicators reveal a west German economy, boosted until recently by massive, deficit-financed transfers to east Germany, that has now shifted to a slower, consolidated, but still positive course. Plummeting GDP, unemployment, and other negative indicators, however, depict a drastically shrinking east German economy that depends increasingly on west German transfers. Self-sustaining growth and development have not yet begun.[2]

Medium- and long-term forecasts for the former GDR are still rare and they differ greatly. Forecasts by E. M. Verkade and by Robert Barro and Xavier Sala-I-Martin, for instance, both contend that catching up with west Germany will be a lengthy process.[3] Verkade predicts that east German jobs will decrease from 9.9 million in 1989 to fewer than 5 million by 1995. This gloomy projection arises despite continued west German transfers of DM 140 billion a year, a 20 percent increase in compensation per employee each year, and an annual 8 percent increase in productivity. Barro and Sala-I-Martin conclude that it will take thirty-five years to close the income gap between east and west by

3

Table 1. Indicators of Macroeconomic Activity in West and East Germany, 1990–93

Indicator	Billions of deutsche marks				Percent change				Percent of GDP			
	1990[a]	1991[a]	1992[b]	1993[b]	1990	1991	1992	1993	1990	1991	1992	1993
West Germany												
GDP	2,417.8	2,612.6	2,762.0	2,858.0	8.7	8.1	6.0	3.5	...	...	...	...
Private consumption	1,321.2	1,420.7	1,493.5	1,558.0	8.2	7.5	5.0	4.5	54.2	54.0	53.9	54.4
Government purchases	444.4	468.1	499.0	512.5	6.1	5.3	6.5	2.5	18.2	17.8	18.0	17.9
Fixed investment	506.8	565.1	596.0	606.5	13.0	11.5	5.5	2.0	20.8	21.5	21.5	21.2
Machinery	234.0	261.6	262.0	255.5	15.0	11.8	0.0	-2.5	9.6	9.9	9.5	8.9
Construction	272.8	303.5	334.0	351.0	11.3	11.3	10.0	5.0	11.2	11.5	12.0	12.3
Change of stocks	3.1	-8.6	-13.0	-3.5	...	...	...	...	0.1	-0.3	-0.5	-0.1
Exports[c]	882.3	1,013.2	1,064.5	1,118.5	11.9	14.8	5.0	5.0	36.2	38.5	38.4	39.1
Imports	718.7	827.2	868.0	929.5	11.7	15.1	5.0	7.0	29.5	31.4	31.3	32.5
Net exports	163.6	186.0	196.0	189.0	...	...	...	...	6.7	7.1	7.1	6.6
GNP	2,439.1	2,631.2	2,771.5	2,862.5	8.4	7.9	5.5	3.5	100	100	100	100
Prices												
GNP	...	...	...	...	3.4	4.1	4.5	3.0	...	...	...	...
Private consumption	...	...	...	...	2.6	3.8	4.0	3.5	...	...	...	...
Government deficit	49.4	93.6	78.5	60.5	...	...	...	...	2.0	3.6	2.8	2.1

East Germany

GDP	227.9	186.2	231.5	276.5	n.a.	−18.3	24.5	19.2	...	...	...	...
Private consumption	159.4	186.7	218.5	239.5	n.a.	17.1	17.0	9.5	69.6	95.5	90.0	82.3
Government purchases	71.0	86.2	105.0	114.5	n.a.	21.5	21.5	9.0	31.0	44.1	43.2	39.3
Fixed investment	61.1	83.0	104.0	129.0	n.a.	35.8	25.0	24.5	26.7	42.5	42.7	44.3
Machinery	20.3	40.4	49.0	58.0	n.a.	98.6	22.0	17.5	8.9	20.7	20.3	19.9
Construction	40.8	42.6	54.5	71.0	n.a.	4.5	28.0	30.5	17.8	21.8	22.5	24.5
Change of stocks	−9.9	2.7	1.0	4.0	n.a.	...	...	...	−4.3	1.4	0.4	1.5
Exports	60.9	60.4	72.0	87.0	n.a.	−0.8	19.0	20.5	26.6	30.9	29.6	29.8
Imports[c]	113.3	223.5	257.0	283.0	n.a.	97.2	15.0	10.0	49.5	114.4	105.8	97.2
Net exports	−52.4	−163.1	−185.0	−196.0	n.a.	...	...	...	−22.9	−83.5	−76.2	−67.4
GNP	229.2	195.4	243.0	291.0	n.a.	−14.7	24.5	20.0	100	100	100	100
Prices												
GNP	...	...	...	...	−3.9	19.1	17.5	11.5	...	...	...	...
Private consumption	...	...	...	...	0	12.8	11.0	8.0	...	...	...	...
Government deficit	12.7	−3.9	18.0	40.5	...	...	...	...	5.9[d]	−2.0[d]	7.4[d]	13.9[d]

Sources: Statistisches Bundesamt, and Rheinisch-Westfälisches Institut für Wirtschaftsforschung (1992).
n.a. Not available.
a. Actual.
b. Projections as of Autumn 1992.
c. Including West German deliveries to East Germany.
d. Percent change of GNP.

Table 2. Employment in West and East Germany, 1990–93

Category	Workers (thousands)				Percent change				Unemployment rate			
	1990	1991	1992	1993	1990	1991	1992	1993	1990	1991	1992	1993
West Germany												
Employed	28,487	29,219	29,470	29,340	3.0	2.6	1.0	−0.5	...	...	...	...
Short-term	56	145	260	450	−48.1	158.9	179.5	173.0	...	...	...	...
Migrators	...	...	...	...	...	...	...	...	...	...	...	...
Commuters	...	...	...	...	...	...	...	...	...	...	...	...
Unemployed	1,883	1,689	1,810	2,115	−7.6	−10.3	7.0	17.0	6.2	5.5	5.8	6.5
East Germany												
Employed	8,868	7,179	6,160	5,875	n.a.	−19.0	−14.0	−4.5	...	...	...	...
Short-term	758	1,617	375	200	n.a.	113.3	−77.8	−46.5	...	...	...	...
Migrators[a]	450	650	770	880	n.a.	44.4	18.5	14.5	...	...	...	...
Commuters	85	315	425	430	n.a.	270.6	35.0	1.0	...	...	...	...
Unemployed	240	913	1,175	1,200	n.a.	280.4	28.5	2.0	2.6	11.3	16.0	17.0

Sources: Statistisches Bundesamt, and Rheinisch-Westfälisches Institut für Wirtschaftsforschung (1992).
n.a. Not available.
a. To west German labor force, cumulative since 1989.

half. They start from a level of west German per capita income double that of east Germany in 1989 and assume a rate of convergence of 2 percent a year (which in turn depends on the productivity of capital and the willingness to save).

Warwick McKibbin offers a more favorable employment outlook.[4] He predicts that 60 percent of the east German labor force will be employed by 1996; the remaining 40 percent, however, will not all find jobs until 2010. Assuming preunification women's labor force participation rates and retirement rates will further decrease, the actual outcome could be significantly "better." The assumptions underlying these results, however, are severe and require decreases in real wages and depreciation of the deutsche mark.

The Institut für Wirtschaftsforschung in Halle presents similar results, projecting that in 2000 east Germany will have 6 million jobs, 4 million of them newly created. The labor potential will be 7.5 million people, with 500,000 commuting to west Germany and 1 million still unemployed.[5] The official Institut für Arbeitsmarkt- und Berufsforschung (IAB) offers an only slightly better forecast, expecting real GDP growth of 11 percent for 1991–92, productivity growth per employee of 11.2 percent, and 6.8 million employed at the end of the century.[6]

Although these projections attempt to clarify trends in a murky situation, all are hindered by limited data and oversimplification. They are based on models that have not yet been tested and that rely very much on assumptions. From the standpoint of economic forecasting, the practical difficulties posed by the east German economy since 1990 recall those presented by west German postwar projections. No model in use in 1945 or 1949 would have been able to predict the later *Wirtschaftswunder* ("economic miracle") or to identify the potential for growth that took place in the 1950s.[7] This observation does not, however, imply that prospects for east German reconstruction can be modeled according to the west German postwar experience.

Apart from these difficulties, there is another fundamental problem. For many years to come, east German development will depend heavily on west Germany's economic growth and, to a lesser extent, on that of the European Community and the world. This dependence not only encompasses west German aid transfers to the east, but also extends to the west's ability to absorb east German job seekers who relocate there (migrants) and east German commuters (see table 2). Development will depend as well on the level of private investment in east Germany. The tendency to overlook these relationships further illustrates the complexity of the new situation and its resistance to economic analysis.

Events and Consequences of the First Two Years

In 1991 east Germany's industrial production had fallen to one-third of its 1989 value; despite massive transfer payments, east German GNP had been reduced by one-third.[8] Full-time employment had been cut in half, mainly at the expense of the elderly and women in what may have been their permanent departure from the labor force. As calculated by the Federal Statistical Office, the GDP of the new Länder came to DM 173 million in 1991 and to DM 45.7 million in the first quarter of 1992. Labor productivity was one-third of west Germany's in 1991, and the effective wage rate reached 50 percent of its western counterpart, yielding east German wage costs some 60 percent higher than the west's. In short, despite huge layoffs, east German production is in no way competitive, even before any consideration of product marketability or quality. In 1991, gross transfers to east Germany rose to DM 139 billion. They are expected to increase to DM 180 billion or DM 200 billion in 1992 and to continue its upward trend. Net transfers—gross transfers adjusted for their macroeconomic effects in west Germany— are about half this size.[9] Transfers that go directly to east German consumption—about two-thirds of all payments—have grown fastest as east German wages approach west German levels and unemployment relief payments increase along with them.

The current dislocations are mostly the consequences of the speed of unification and the way it was implemented.[10] From a purely economic point of view, a gradualist approach starting in early 1990 would have been preferable. But once the borders between the Germanies were opened on November 9, 1989, political, economic, and social events cascaded, and any hope of a gradual transition vanished.[11] With the collapse of the Berlin Wall came free movement to west Germany for east Germans—for many this was the first time they had known such freedom. The mobility allowed the unrelenting exposure of the divergent political, economic, social, cultural, and humanitarian conditions in the two parts of Germany, a divergence to which the populace of both west and east sought an immediate end.

Realistically speaking, there was no alternative to the rapid pace of reunification. Nothing short of a decision by the west to reseal the border could have slowed it, and the FRG's Basic Law (Grundgesetz), with its guarantee of free mobility as well as its mandate toward reunification, precluded any such action. Although the two Germanies had adopted the relationship of two independent states and the GDR had been granted diplomatic recognition with the Basic Treaty (Grundlagenvertrag) of the early 1970s, west German Basic Law never ceased to grant the GDR's citizens full FRG citizenship. The federal government and all major parties accurately assessed the chance for unification posed by this window of opportunity.

The west German government acted quickly and effectively to address the foreign policy and security policy issues stemming from unification, in particular the adoption of the rights of the allies in the GDR and international recognition of the enlarged FRG. The action received the full support of the U.S. and Soviet leadership. Far less auspicious was west German handling of the deep economic, social, and cultural disparities with east Germany. In public at least they were continually underestimated, if not ignored or suppressed. This behavior may partly be ascribed to electoral politics—federal elections were slated for December 1990—as well as to a collective misjudgment of the state of the GDR's economy and the resources needed for its rebuilding, realities that only hit home after July 1, 1990, when the Monetary, Economic, and Social Union was enacted.[12]

The result of more than forty years of communist central planning, domineering state control, and public ownership exceeded even the worst expectations.

—Large-scale production was uneven because of the centrally planned autarky and the frequent shortages of industrial inputs.

—Capital stock was outdated and poorly designed.

—Production and market-oriented service industries and repair and maintenance had been neglected.

—Government, educational, and cultural institutions were overstaffed.

—Regional monostructures had been imposed, resulting in complete regional breakdowns once the monostructures were shaken.

—The environment was heavily damaged.

—Infrastructure, especially transportation and telecommunications, was sorely deficient.

—Local and regional institutional infrastructure had deteriorated and local administration had collapsed.

—Workers and skills were out of balance: training in industry, science and technology, and ideology had been overemphasized, and all other fields had been discriminated against.

—Structural paralysis, stagnating modernization efforts, and the absence of innovations and of incentives to introduce them were pervasive.

—The population was inexperienced in market-oriented behavior.

—The labor force was unmotivated.

—There were too few entrepreneurs and self-employed business people, which if measured by FRG standards should have equaled 900,000 persons, and business was generally biased toward providing consumer goods and serving the household sector.

Before July 1990 most observers assumed the GDR had certain strengths that would allow it to catch up quickly.[13] The training and qualifications of the work force did not appear very different from west Germany's, and education and professional schooling in the two states also seemed to have much in common. It was well known that the GDR's growth owed more to increases in the labor force than to increases in labor productivity. Capital-intensive industries were overrepresented (though the GDR claimed to have succeeded in raising labor productivity by 6 percent annually).[14] In addition, the GDR was presumed to have an excellent product mix and the marketing expertise necessary to conquer east European markets. Surprisingly, west German observers realized the dim prospects for the GDR economy only after unification. The GDR's industrial planners themselves seemed to have recognized these deficiencies only in 1989, whereupon they concluded that the GDR would become insolvent internationally by the end of 1990.

The swift and complete opening of the closed society and economy in July 1990 failed to bring the rapid change and improvement that had been widely expected. Instead problems worsened. The old order had been inefficient, but at least within limits it had worked. The new order imposed by the union, with its complex system of laws, institutions, and customs developed over dozens of years in the FRG, hardly reflected the needs of a reborn east Germany.[15] It also quickly became clear that a mere declaration of a market economy was not enough: ingrained attitudes and habits had to be overcome, market behavior learned, and motivation nurtured. All this required a transfer of knowledge and experience, and far more time, than was ever expected.

The cultural shock of the new order was not the only one east Germany had to absorb. No less disruptive was the opening of its

10

markets to international trade and exchange rates. East German goods suddenly had to compete with those of the highly advanced Western economies, both in third countries and in the domestic market. The introduction of the deutsche mark as the official currency sacrificed all chance of buffering price and cost disparities through exchange rate manipulation—in stark contrast to the practices of other former Eastern bloc countries. For the producers of tradable goods this was a disaster: the 400 percent revaluation of the east German mark meant an instant loss of competitiveness of all internationally traded goods and services in all markets, including the Eastern bloc countries and west Germany.[16] Despite this loss, however, west Germany seems to have recovered a considerable portion of east Germany's former share: west German exports to the east increased from 46 percent of German exports to Eastern Europe in 1989 (DM 24.5 billion) to 71 percent in 1991 (DM 26.0 billion), while imports from the east soared from 42 percent (DM 19.2 billion) to 80 percent (DM 26.4 billion) of the total German imports from Eastern Europe.[17]

Although the economy of post–World War II West Germany is at times presumed to be comparable with that of east Germany following the signing of the MESU, this sketch of the east German economy has indicated some of the main differences. A comparison of key economic indicators confirms the disparity (figure 1). But it should not be forgotten that despite the strong upward trends in the FRG after the war, economists at the time urged caution, and a massive housing program prepared by the federal government in 1950 to stabilize production failed to be implemented only because the Korean War increased demand for exports from the German and European economies.

Even when the sparseness and age of the capital stock and its damages are removed from consideration, the west German start was hampered by only twelve years of national socialism, and the postwar interregnum had lasted only three. The economy suffered because of the war and postwar damage and disruption, but the foundations were intact: government institutions at the state and local level, including the judiciary, still existed. Restoration took place almost naturally—to the dismay of those who had longed for an absolutely new start instead of reconstruction.[18] To characterize West Germany's post–World War II situation as a zero hour is misleading. Such a point never exists: not in 1945–48 West Germany and not in 1989–90 east Germany. The starting point is always formed by the experience, knowledge, and perceptions

Figure 1. Economic Development, West Germany 1948–53, and East Germany, 1990–92

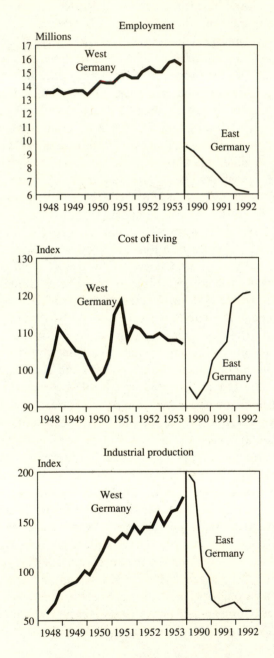

12

Figure 1. (*continued*)

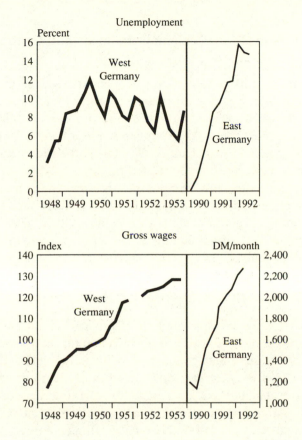

Sources: Federal Statistical Office, Federal Employment Agency, and Werner Abelshauser, "Die ordnungspolitische Epochenbedeutung der Weltwirtschaftskrise in Deutschland," in Dietmar Petzina, ed., *Ordnungspolitische Weichenstellungen nach dem Zweiten Weltkrieg* (Berlin: Duncker und Humblot, 1991), pp. 11 ff.

of the acting generation, the historical components of the present. This holds in particular in a situation such as the one in 1990, when the GDR deliberately sought to join the west German course.

The Nature of the Problem: Complexity and Contradiction

During the intensive debate over how to achieve German unification in the first months of 1990, many economists reduced the problem to that of transforming a centrally planned economy into a market economy. Because the circumstances were unanimously considered unprecedented, criticism seemed ruled out and sober analysis barred.[19] But managing the socioeconomic problems of German unification required distinguishing at least five closely related tasks:

—integrating the east German into the west German economy, and hence into the European Community and the world economy;

—creating the public and private conditions to facilitate supply, particularly physical infrastructure, which is necessary to vitalize the east German economy;

—liberalizing the economic sector;

—taking into account rapidly shifting public preferences vis-à-vis the environment and the public sector in general;

—confronting the daunting task of privatizing and returning property to former owners or compensating them for their losses, including satisfying the state-held companies' outstanding debts (*Altschulden*).

Such a classification suggests that when unification is seen as a collection of separate tasks, precedents for carrying them out might well be found. More specifically, there have been enlargements of territory before, and attempts to revitalize national economies, liberalizations and deregulations of economies, drastic shifts of preferences, and the need to compensate property losses sometimes dating far into the past. To what extent can such examples guide the present?

Precedents for Restructuring

The German unification of 1871 is one potential precedent for economic integration.[20] In 1871, however, areas brought together were already largely integrated (Prussia, Zollverein, Norddeutscher Bund). There already existed a tremendous volume of trade among them. Furthermore, the differences among the states forming the German Empire in

14

1871 were comparatively small. Prussia, the largest of them, with almost two-thirds of the empire's population, territory, and economic capacity, contained greater economic extremes within its borders than existed among the several German states. Finally, government and governmental regulations were only a minor part of life—the government's share of GNP was about 10 percent, and 70 percent of that went to military and general administration expenses.

A second potential model is the integration of the Saar region into the Federal Republic in 1957. The Saar had been severed from Germany from 1918 to 1935 and again from the end of World War II until 1957. The Saarland at that time had only 1 million citizens and, despite twelve years of French rule, it retained a great deal in common with west Germany. But even though a transition period of two and one-half years preceded full monetary union, the strains of reintegration are still visible.

There are few successful examples of economic vitalization despite the recent, often simplistic, reduction of vitalization to the mere introduction of a market economy. Again, the *Wirtschaftswunder* may seem the natural comparison. Even many who maintained that the GDR's situation was unique drew this parallel and used the growth rates the FRG had experienced in 1950–70 as a yardstick to determine the rate at which east Germany would catch up.[21] These growth rates were, however, accompanied by a generally high demand for goods, low expectations, an undervalued currency, few opportunities to emigrate, the Marshall Plan's initial financial assistance, and, under the GATT, the opening of the U.S. market to European exports.[22] These extenuating circumstances are largely ignored in discussions of the problems of transition and playing catch-up in Eastern European countries, except perhaps as they concern agriculture.[23]

The remaking of a society is not the work of simply presenting alternatives. Examples of sudden shifts in popular preferences and the strategies to cope with them are rare if one excludes the recent insistence on market economies over socialist economies. A more typical example might be the implementation of comprehensive environmental policies in the FRG. But these were debated at length and took more than twenty-five years to bring about. And few societies have undergone a more thorough reconstruction that the one Germany is attempting. Even the restoration of the former legitimate French monarchy in 1815, for instance, did not lead to attempts to restore private or feudal property existing before 1789 or to compensate for its loss.

Germany has decided to provide restitution or compensation for private property appropriated by the state since 1945, and this poses a seemingly insurmountable obstacle to a fresh start. In the diplomatic negotiations on unification, the Soviet Union required (as had the last democratically elected government of the GDR) that the legal results achieved after World War II by the Soviet administration or its east German administrators remain intact.[24] For all other cases, however, the principal decision was to restore property in kind. Compensation for property loss was to take precedence only if new investments in the public interest would otherwise be hindered. Because of this proviso, more than 2.1 million cases will have to be decided; in Berlin alone more than 100,000 cases are pending.[25] The courts will be swamped for years deciding these matters. A mere 5 percent of cases have been settled so far, and for certain types of cases the present regulations may not even prove final.[26] Another grave mistake was the failure to eliminate outstanding debts of the state-owned companies. These had hardly any bearing on companies' assets, and for most it was clear that the companies could not even earn the interest payments. Oddly enough, if the Treuhandanstalt, the east German privatization agency, sells a company, its debts are canceled outright.

The Treuhandanstalt

As an observer of the early privatizations in Poland remarked, "it is much easier taking from one and giving to all than it's going to be taking from all and giving back to one."[27] This holds entirely true for the privatization of public property in Germany, as the history and performance of the Treuhandanstalt illustrate.[28] The institution was founded March 1, 1990, four months before enactment of the MESU, to supervise the state-owned enterprises. By June it had received the mandate to reorganize and privatize these companies. After October 3 privatization of 8,000 companies (excluding retail firms, restaurants, and so forth) with 45,000 production units became its primary goal. It also planned to shut down unproductive operations, such as uranium mining.

From the start, however, the Treuhandanstalt's activities suffered from the conflict between the goals of privatization on one hand and reorganization and streamlining on the other. The agency tried to resolve the conflict by combining privatization with rules requiring

16

buyers to make promises as to the number of jobs to be saved. Recently, demands have also been made that regional policy requirements be taken into account or that small- and medium-sized enterprises be made to take greater risks in the privatization process.[29] Although any short-term commitment of buyers is not worth very much, long-term commitments will be difficult to secure if payment of a penalty for not fulfilling the contract will cause bankruptcy. Fortunately, this is not yet a problem; only 10 percent of job and investment pledges have been broken. More generally, it should also be realized that many west German buyers may have only a limited interest in encouraging competitors.[30] Their main motives seem to be to gain easy market access and establish the necessary capacity to serve the new market. In other words, for now the creation of export-based growth poles to earn the necessary income from outside the region seems to be an exception.

The Treuhandanstalt has been criticized, among other things, for selling property below the true market value. Of course, given the limited time and ample supply of international companies to be privatized (ranging from some based in Argentina to those in the eastern republics of the former Soviet Union), this may well have been the case. In addition, because only privatized companies seem to invest, to be able to gain a market position, and hence to provide the permanent jobs so badly needed, some compromise may have been found. Since early 1992 the Treuhandanstalt seems to be more inclined to restructure.

By June 1, 1992, the Treuhandanstalt had 4,000 employees in 15 offices that had privatized 7,600 companies and production units and 7,000 smaller possessions (retail shops, restaurants, and so on), for which it received DM 29.3 billion. In addition, investors made DM 138.5 billion worth of investment commitments, representing some 1.2 million jobs. Most of the acquisitions were made by west Germans. Foreigners bought 350 firms with about DM 10.8 billion in investments and commitments to provide 100,000 jobs. With some 4 million employees in Treuhand properties in mid-1990 and about 1 million in mid-1992, and 1.2 million job commitments from the new proprietors, privatization implied a loss of nearly 2 million jobs (see note 28).

Of course, it was not privatization but the lack of the firms' competitiveness that caused these losses. The cost of privatization has amounted in all to DM 77.5 billion as of 1992: DM 30.2 billion for guarantees, DM 18 billion for such expenditures as fiscal aid, credits, and interest payments on debts incurred during the GDR period (*Altschulden*), as

17

well as the assumption of these debts in the opening balances or acknowledgment of compensation claims. The distribution of the companies privatized across the east German Länder only varies from 70 percent in Berlin to about 55 percent in Thuringia. A similar evenness seems to hold for the sectoral distribution of the companies.

The Treuhandanstalt's performance leads the agency to expect that it may finish its sales activities in 1993, one year ahead of the original schedule. It could then operate on a much smaller scale and concentrate on enforcing the buyers' commitments to invest and create jobs. It will be burdened with debts of about DM 300 billion, of which DM 200 billion would be the result of the assumption of *Altschulden*, environmental commitments, and so on.

The size of this negative balance is also determined by the mechanics of the other fund regulating the net worth of the GDR—the Kreditabwicklungsfonds—that comprises both the old debts of the GDR in foreign exchange (transfer rubles) and the initial capital of banks and others in their opening balances, amounting to DM 140 billion. This does not even account for the other heritage of the GDR—the converted loans to the housing sector, comprising some DM 50 billion, initially to be assumed by the new owners. (The first estimates of the Modrow government in early 1990 set a net capital worth of the GDR's industrial property of about DM 1.2 trillion, later reduced by the last GDR government between DM 800 and DM 600 billion, and revised by the federal government to DM 400 billion in October 1990.)

According to the Unification Treaty, the debts of the Treuhandanstalt are supposed to be divided between the federal government and the new east German Länder, though with their expected fiscal difficulties this is not likely to happen. Furthermore, even if the Treuhand ends its sales activities in 1994, it will not have sold all the firms. Companies representing several hundred thousand employees will likely prove unmarketable, and their prospects are unclear.

Summary of Problems

To sum up, German unification has been unique in two respects. First, although there are some historical precedents for the various elements of the current German situation, they differ considerably in their specifics and their circumstances. Nevertheless, examining these differences would have improved the understanding of present dilemmas.

Second the unification process has been complex because of the large number of different but closely linked problems and tasks. Though in the longer term some of these problems may turn out to be assets (the modernization of the capital stock and the environmental cleanup, for instance),[31] in the short term they form a massive stumbling block. Dealing with most of these problems, even one at a time, is no simple matter, as the uneven regional distribution of prosperity in Europe and worldwide attests.[32] Ultimately, most of the policy problems and policy goals related to unification are in conflict with one another, at least in the short term, particularly under the current conditions of limited resources.[33] The same is true of the choice of policy instruments, where trade-offs exist that should have been studied before setting priorities.

Whether institutional measures such as the establishment of a special federal ministry of reconstruction would have helped is not clear. The GDR's negotiators repeatedly asked for such an Aufbauministerium as part of the Treaty of Unification.[34] The idea was raised again at the creation of the first all-German government in early 1991, and now the Christian Democratic deputies from the eastern Länder are demanding a state minister in the chancellor's office. Some of the conflicts between the many goals and policies would, no doubt, have surfaced much faster if the ministry had been established, and political responsibility would have been more in line with the democratic need for accountability.

This view of the complexity of German unification is not widely shared. The public's understanding of the complexity, linkages, and trade-offs between certain tasks and goals has, however, improved somewhat. People now understand that a rapid catching-up in east German living standards conflicts with the reconstruction of the economic base, because abruptly higher wages would discourage investors or because the limited fiscal means would be diverted from improving the capital stock, though even here there is a conflict between consumption goals (such as additional housing) and improved production. But in general, the conflicting nature of the tasks and the restrictions on resources and time under which they had to be solved have rarely been realized.

Hence, the political leadership has hardly developed or considered priorities. The prevailing view was that a revitalization effort launched in parallel with a generous initial endowment would suffice. Economic difficulties, such as rising unemployment, sluggish investment, and insufficient new Länder revenues, would be settled by applying routine legal procedures or administrative measures. In the early months, before the start of the MESU and shortly thereafter, this misperception was understandable. But with the growing awareness of the limited financial and real resources and increasing unemployment, such simplistic assumptions no longer suffice. It seems clear that there is no quick fix; nor is a long-term perspective easy to discover.

The Cost of the Cure: Unification's Fiscal Conditions

In the first year, discussions of the economics of unification focused on short-term macroeconomic, fiscal, and monetary implications and only differed insofar as underlying assumptions were concerned.[35] But since the scope and time horizons of these deliberations have been extended, economists now try to integrate supply-side reactions, wage reactions, and monetary policy.[36] The real economic and production implications of unification for east Germany, given the loss of its old structures of supply and demand and the long-term repercussions of the west German transfers on its own economy, are still largely ignored. Why is there such a fiscal bias in analysis and policy?

First, the widespread view inside and outside government held that unification was mainly, if not exclusively, a matter of financial means, with the amount to be determined from unspecified west German production functions for private and public goods. This belief led to policy's nearly exclusive reliance on fiscal action. (See the appendix for a list of these measures. Interestingly, most of the few measures in the nonfinancial sector consisted in postponements or modifications of previous understandings.) Problems in the nonfinancial sphere were relegated to the Treuhandanstalt or to west Germany's private sector.

Second, unification became a reality at the start of a worldwide recession. The international community, hoping for lower interest rates, nervously awaited the effects on the capital market of huge transfers to east Germany and the resulting west German deficits. The implications for world trade, or at least for European trade, were overlooked. For the European Community's GNP growth rate in 1990 and 1991, an additional 0.5 and 0.7 percentage points were calculated.[37]

A third, more technical aspect is that the fiscal effects of a government's economic transactions are the first to show up. They are expressed in numerical terms and can easily be transformed into illustrative figures. In other words, the fiscal bias in part reflects Western

20

ignorance of the working of the supply side in general and under east German conditions in particular, and a naive optimism that supply-side problems will solve themselves.

So far, all published official estimates of the fiscal costs of unification have proved much too low, as have most private ones (table 3). A major reason was the unrealistically high estimate of east German productivity and competitiveness. Thus the drastic decline of east German production after the MESU was severely underestimated. Another factor was the unrealistic conversion rate of east German marks into deutsche marks. In this context, however, the breakdown of large parts of the east European markets should be mentioned; these had absorbed as much as 70 percent of east German exports, which, ignoring the linkages of the export industries, accounted for 20 percent of its GNP.[38]

Another often overlooked reason for the low estimates is that the legal framework of unification and the consequent fiscal needs of east Germany could be accurately judged only after the establishment of the MESU and the ratification of the Treaty of Unification by the two German parliaments in September 1990.[39] Even then, neither the number nor the size of fiscal obligations related to unification could be completely foreseen, at least not outside government. This is at least partly confirmed by Wolfgang Schaeuble, the West German minister of the interior in charge of negotiating the Unification Treaty. Schaeuble claimed that if, in the summer of 1990, a realistic picture of the fiscal burdens to come had been made public, the West German electorate and parliament's acceptance of rapid unification would have been jeopardized. In addition, politicans had full trust in the potential of the west German economy to cope with the problems to come.[40] Whatever the reasons, in the end the fiscal requirements caused no trouble—other than a second jump in the capital market interest rates, the first occurring after the collapse of the Berlin Wall in autumn 1989—in the financial markets after February 1990, when Chancellor Helmut Kohl announced the plan for the MESU.

Current Fiscal Involvement

Quantifying the fiscal needs of the new German Länder (including east Berlin) or the transfers required of the west German Länder is still risky because all forecasts are, to an unusually high degree, open ended. Neither the dimensions of the problems nor the time needed to solve

Table 3. Macroeconomic Forecasts for West and East Germany, by Indicator, 1989–93[a]

Indicator	1989				1990				1991				1992			1993
	I	II	III	Actual	I	II	III	Actual	I	II	III	Actual	I	II	III	I
West Germany																
GNP/Real (percent change)	4.0	3.0	4.0	4.0	3.0	3.75	4.0	4.9	2.5	2.5	3.5	3.6	2.0	1.0	1.0	0.5
Prices (percent change)	2.5	3.0	3.5	3.1	3.0	3.0	2.5	2.6	4.0	3.5	3.5	3.8	4.0	3.75	4.0	3.5
Unemployment (thousands)	2,300	2,075	2,030	2,038	2,000	1,950	1,900	1,883	2,000	1,680	1,700	1,689	1,700	1,780	1,800	2,030
Government deficit (billions of deutsche marks)	14.5	6.0	0	-2.8	17.0	20.0	57.5	49.4	82.5	79.0	56.5	93.6	40.5	(101.5)[b]	(95.5)[b]	(10.00)[b]
East Germany																
GNP/Real (percent change)	n.a.	n.a.	n.a.	n.a.	n.a.	n.a.	-14.5[c]	-15.7	-5.0[c]	-17.5	-22.5	-28.4	13.5	10.5	5.5	7.0
Prices (percent change)	n.a.	n.a.	n.a.	n.a.	n.a.	n.a.	n.a.	0.9	n.a.	11.0	12.0	12.8	12.0	12.5	11.0	8.5
Unemployment (thousands)	n.a.	n.a.	n.a.	n.a.	n.a.	n.a.	250	240	1,400	1,200	950	913	1,400	1,350	1,190	1,240
Government deficit (billions of deutsche marks)	n.a.	n.a.	n.a.	n.a.	n.a.	n.a.	13.5	12.7	7.5	34.5	31.5	3.9	52.5	n.a.	n.a.	n.a.

Sources: Arbeitsgemeinschaft deutscher wirtschaftswissenschaftlicher Forschungsinstitute, *Die Lage der Weltwirtschaft und der deutschen Wirtschaft im Herbst [Frühjar] 1990 [1991]* (Essen, 1990, 1991); and data from Statistisches Bundesamt for 1992.

n.a. Not available.

a. I: estimates in autumn, previous year. II: estimates in spring, current year. III: estimates in autumn, current year. Actual: as of Autumn 1992.

c. Current prices.

b. Unified Germany.

them has been ascertained. Since political unification, much of the legal framework now appears to be clear. However, east German economic development, which depends directly (unemployment assistance, for instance) or indirectly (to compensate for its low tax revenues) on transfers, is hardly predictable. Furthermore, the legal and administrative framework, which determines fiscal requirements, is still being modified.[41]

With the exception of a large number of investment subsidies, there were two programs specifically designed to motivate investment. The first called for the establishment of two major investment funds. The German Unity Fund (Fonds Deutsche Einheit) was founded in May 1990. It was financed jointly by federal and western Länder governments (with DM 22 billion for the second half of 1990, climbing to DM 35 billion in 1991, and gradually diminishing so that after 1995 no new distributions of tax receipts and revenues have been fixed for all of Germany). The Gemeinschaftswerk Aufschwung Ost (Joint Program Upswing East) was established in March 1991 (DM 12 billion in 1991). Typically the need for the second fund was discovered very late. The funds' pivotal function in the new Länder can easily be realized: most other funds were intended for purposes other than investment.

Another program designed to motivate investment called for subsidized credits for private enterprises and local communities in the new Länder. The credits were to be provided mainly by funds from the revolving European Recovery Program (ERP), which is still in existence, and the federal government's special credit institutions, in particular the Kreditanstalt für Wiederaufbau and the Deutsche Ausgleichsbank. In 1991 they granted DM 21 billion in loans. Because these loans had to be matched by investors, the sum stimulated may total DM 40 billion to DM 50 billion, or three-quarters of all investment in east Germany.

In 1990, transfers from west to east Germany amounted to DM 45 billion, more than 90 percent of which went for payments to states and communities and for unemployment assistance. Meanwhile the share of consumption expeditures represented by these transfers seems to have been reduced to 60 percent (table 4). Of course, from an east German perspective the transfers are not handouts. For some transfers (health care and pensions) recipients have made contributions; others, such as the payments from the German Unity Fund, are financed by credits, and east Germans will have to contribute something to its annuity. In 1991

Table 4. Financial Transfers to East Germany, 1990–94
Billions of deutsche marks

Component	Year				
	1990	*1991*	*1992*	*1993*	*1994*
Transfer payments to Länder					
and local communities[a]	43.5	111.3	125.5	120.5	n.a.
German Unity Fund	22.0	35.0	34.0	31.5	23.5
Joint Program Upswing East	. . .	12.0	12.0	n.a.	n.a.
Unification-related					
federal expenditures	19.2	50.5	62.5	71.0	85.0
VAT compensation of Länder	1.3	10.8	12.0	13.0	14.0
Transfer payments by west					
German Länder[b]	1.0	2.0	2.5	3.0	3.0
Unification-related revenue					
losses in west Germany[c]	. . .	1.0	2.5	2.0	1.5
Transfer payments to the east					
German social security system	2.7	20.5	39.5	40.5	42.5
Unemployment insurance system	1.9	20.5	35.5	34.5	35.0
Old age pension system	0.8	. . .	2.0	6.0	7.5
Gross fiscal transfer payments	46.2	131.8	163.0	161.0	167.0
Additional (net) tax and social					
security revenues in					
west Germany[d]	15.1	57.0	63.4	53.5	53.5
Expenditure cuts of division-					
related costs	4.0	5.7	11.4	16.4	21.0
Net fiscal transfer payments	27.1	69.1	88.2	91.1	92.5

Sources: Author's computations. Figures are rounded.
n.a. Not available.
a. Excluding interest subsidies for European Recovery Program loans.
b. Excluding structural aid.
c. Because of tax incentives for investments in east Germany.
d. Econometric model results, based on the assumption of no unification-caused expenditures and revenue increases.

and 1992 transfers were DM 130.5 billion and DM 155 billion, respectively. These sums account for two-thirds of east Germany's GNP, or more than DM 9,900 per capita in east Germany and DM 2,400 per capita in west Germany. Net unemployment assistance totaled DM 25.5 billion in 1991 and DM 32 billion in 1992. The amount spent on public investment, mostly construction, was DM 13 billion in 1991 and DM 20 billion in 1992.[42]

The deficit in the government sector—federal, state, and local communities and the social security system (the national accounts)—rose from DM 69.4 billion in 1990 to DM 94.4 billion in 1991, and will reach

DM 101.5 billion in 1992. Despite increases in taxes and social security contributions of DM 30 billion in 1991 and DM 40 billion in 1992 and cuts in subsidies of DM 10 billion a year, the deficit was expected to be about 3.4 percent of GNP in 1991 and 1992. Taking into account expenditures outside the budget and binding government obligations such as those of the Treuhandanstalt (projected at DM 30 billion in 1992), the all-German government deficit in 1992 could well reach DM 130 billion to DM 140 billion. A significant component is the adjustment of east German pensions to west German levels, which will cost nearly DM 20 billion. Adding the deficits of the federal postal system, the federal railway system, and the east German railway system—DM 30 billion in all—total government sector obligations of DM 160 billion to DM 170 billion are not inconceivable. This would come to about 5 percent of GNP. By comparison, Marshall Plan transfers to west Germany from 1948 to 1952 amounted to 2 percent of German GNP.

There is little doubt that deficit figures of these magnitudes are at the maximum that a democratic society can currently sustain.[43] Moreover, there is a great deal of fiscal inflexibility that makes these levels all the more untenable. The government sector's interest payments, still excluding some east German shadow households (which have to be integrated into the budgets by 1995 at the latest), are approaching DM 100 billion. These payments are bound to increase considerably. The current government debt and an 8 percent interest rate are expected to consume 12 to 15 percent of the government sector's income by the turn of the century. In 1991 this level was 6 percent.[44] And about two-thirds of the transfers to east Germany are entitlements and hence difficult to control.

Recent reallocations, though larger than previous ones, only amount to DM 50 billion, or 2 percent of GNP. Taking into account the announced 1 percent increase in value-added tax in 1993, this would amount to 2.3 percent. The 1983 budget cuts, the largest to date in the FRG, amounted to 2 percent of GNP. Yet even though the combined tax and social security contribution reached an all-time high of 43.3 percent of GNP in 1992, further reallocation is still needed because of unification. Those who were skeptical that the DM 35 billion a year that had previously been spent on so-called division-related costs (Berlin aid, assistance to west German areas bordering on the east, defense expenditures, and so forth) would be quickly made available for other purposes were proven right, though by 1994 division-related costs may

25

well be reduced by DM 25 billion. Equally disappointing, the federal government, despite all its unprecedented fiscal demands, made few of the significant cuts in subsidies it had announced in early 1991.[45] These policy difficulties result not only from political constraints but also from the very different requirements in east and west Germany.

Nevertheless, by 1994 Germany's government deficit could again dip below 3 percent because tax elasticity is still about 1.07 despite the tax reforms of the 1980s.[46] This, however, means abandoning the planned restitution of tax receipts caused by fiscal drag and the remaining part of the planned DM 25 billion to DM 30 billion reduction of business taxes. Moreover, not all future fiscal obligations have been quantified or accurately accounted for and could easily add another DM 45 billion to the public debt.[47]

The uncertainties implicit in development in east Germany could drive the deficits of the Treuhandanstalt beyond present expectations. Similarly, there are risks arising from international obligations and demands: the economic stabilization of the east European countries and the former Soviet republics and increasing commitments to the European Community to bolster the structural fund and establish the cohesion fund for economic development in the weaker member countries.[48]

Crowding Out?

Deficits of this magnitude raise strong concerns that government borrowing will crowd out private borrowing. However, the first two years of deficit spending at unprecedented levels have not confirmed such concerns. Following the results of econometric models, about 1.5 to 2.0 percentage points of the 4.5 percent GNP growth in 1990 and of the 3.1 percent growth in 1991 must be attributed to the unification-related deficit spending, accounting for 300,000 to 400,000 of the 800,000 new jobs created in west Germany in 1991–92.[49] Somewhat surprising was the reduced unemployment rate. Of those who found jobs in 1990, about 40 percent came from the long-term unemployed; the figure is usually closer to 20 percent.[50] This trend continued through most of 1991, and for the first time in fifteen years the number of long-term unemployed workers was halved. This clearly was the effect of the transfers to east Germany in particular sectors (retail trade) and regions (those parts of west Germany near the former intra-German border), combined with the flexible employment and wage behavior of immigrants.

The weight of each factor is hard to determine, however. Econometric models indicate that the 1.5 million immigrants to the FRG from 1988 to 1991, of whom 900,000 were from east Germany, helped produce a 5 percent higher real GNP, lowered inflation by 0.5 percent, and reduced the public deficit by DM 13 billion.[51]

The effects of deficit spending on prices were small at first, as could be expected from a cost-determined price development, and costs have not yet been much affected. Significant price increases have been limited to a few sectors, mainly construction, which is hardly an effect of the transfers to east Germany. However, the capital markets showed early and marked reaction (figure 2). Yields on outstanding bonds jumped 1 percentage point to 9 percent in the first quarter of 1990, when the principal agreement between the two German governments was reached but before any serious forecast of the coming fiscal burden for west Germany and its financing could be made. So although the basic market reaction proved correct (signaling a significant increase in real interest rates), the interest elasticity of capital turned out to be much higher than previously assumed.[52] However, the final effect of increased government deficits on interest rates has yet to be felt. At the same time, the underestimation of the financial system's elasticity to monetary shocks was reminiscent of the interest rate reductions in the United States in the early 1980s, when tax cuts caused the government deficit to balloon.[53]

A widespread destabilizing of the economy, however, has been registered since the second half of 1991. The subsiding of the increased demand stimulated by unification led to an economic slowdown. Inflationary pressures were created by high wage settlements unaccompanied by productivity gains and by increased consumer taxes, which alone were responsible for a 0.75 percent increase in inflation. No compromise in wage or fiscal policy was offered to help achieve the newly set stability requirements. These tendencies threatened to undermine the economic foundations of the new Germany.

As a consequence, the Bundesbank felt compelled to demonstrate its determination to achieve stability. It set monetary targets that gave no room to inflationary expectations. To curb the unexpectedly high monetary growth, it raised interest rates several times.[54] Although the Bundesbank was accused of choking west German expansion and delaying the turnaround of the rest of Europe, the capital markets seemed to respect its firm stand. Long-term interest rates fell slightly

Figure 2. Typical Long-Term Interest Rates in OECD Countries, 1985–92

Percent

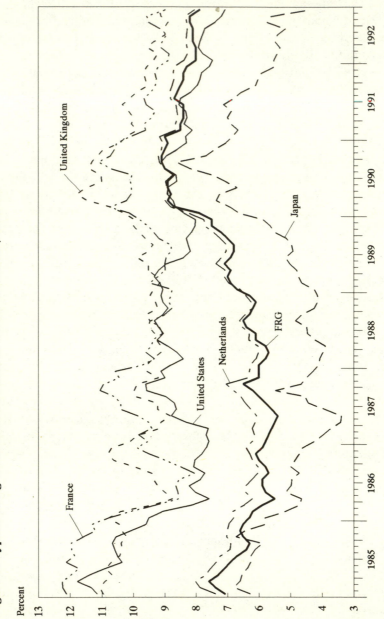

Source: OECD, *Financial Statistics* (Paris, 1992)

in reaction to the increase in the discount rate in December 1991, and Germany's investment climate seemed hardly to have been affected. In the first two quarters of 1992 the west German business cycle appeared more robust than in similar stages of previous cycles, although in the second half of the year the economy was approaching stagnation.

Nevertheless, the government sector's large capital needs put a great deal of stress on the capital markets. Although the average tax rate and social security contribution together exceed 43 percent of GNP, only one-third of these unification-related expenditures have been cashed in by the government sector through higher tax and social security revenues in the past three years (see table 4).[55]

Neither the federal government nor the Länder or local governments have done much to improve the outlook. The federal government, the main player, has failed to present a firm assessment of future fiscal needs, a plan outlining how they should be financed (taxes, expenditure cuts, debt) and by whom (persons, groups, generations, programs), and a way to improve growth conditions. Of course, the unions must support the stability policy as well. So far, this has been true only to a limited degree, as certified by the 1991 wage settlements in the public sector and the strikes during the 1992 wage round.

Distributional Decisions

Although tight monetary and fiscal policy seem inevitable for the next few years, the fiscal burdens certainly could be distributed more broadly and evenly. For example, the DM 20 billion increase in government sector income in early 1991 was created by increasing social security contribution rates in lieu of increasing taxes. But civil servants as well as the self-employed (about 5 million people) are mostly exempt from social security contributions, and thus from an increase. The March 1991 tax package, including the value-added tax increase of January 1, 1993, has certain biases too: the 7.5 percent surcharge on income tax was limited to twelve months, but the increase in indirect taxes has no limitation. This has particular relevance for east Germany, where for the next few years most tax revenues will be from indirect taxes. Higher indirect taxes also increase the inflation rate. In 1992, administrative price hikes caused a 1 percent increase in inflation, which gave wage claims an additional push of 0.5 to 0.7 percent.

There is no doubt that with present policy constraints and investments this is not the hour for exercises in income redistribution. There is room, however, for more equitable burden sharing than now prevails.

The Impact of the Cure: Transfers, Capital, and Labor

Before we examine problems of the nonfinancial sector, some remarks on the general perception of the problem are in order. For many economists the transformation and vitalization of the east German economy are described by the production function, or more precisely, the west German production function. Leaving east German capital stock out of the equation, the amount of capital necessary to create efficient full employment was calculated. The most favorable investment ratios generated totals of DM 1.3 trillion to DM 2.0 trillion. Building a modern stock of capital on that order cannot be achieved in a couple of years, and the restructuring process is now presumed to require at least ten to fifteen years.[56] A detailed discussion of the analytical merits of the production function is beyond the scope of this analysis, but economists now recognize that this concept was useless in judging the economic performance of the Eastern bloc, and postwar and present evidence seems to argue against its appropriateness under current circumstances.[57]

Neither is the role of the entrepreneur adequately taken into account, and it does not seem possible to clearly determine the capacity of the existing capital stock or the investment necessary for its modernization.[58] Diagnostic and prognostic difficulties of this type also make it difficult to pursue exclusively either a growth-oriented or a maintenance-oriented strategy to revive east Germany's economy. While the first strategy will lead quickly to competitive production, it may also be associated with a high rate of unemployment besides being very costly, and not just in a fiscal sense. The second strategy, subsidizing existing firms, may be less costly, but it may block any initiative for the required fundamental changes.[59]

Just as there are limits to the diversion of west German fiscal resources to east Germany, absorption and transfer problems limit the benefits the east can obtain from west German aid.

Before going into a more detailed discussion of these problems, we should clarify two far-reaching factors. First, east Germany is part of the European and world markets. No room exists for any special way, except for temporary measures by the European Community, to help east Germany adapt smoothly to its new regulatory framework. World markets tend to require products that meet high technical, quality, and environmental standards and are characterized by capital-intensive production. Making east Germany competitive is a huge task for employers, administrators, and management and for the capital stock and infrastructure. The FRG's traditional mode of economic assistance has been oriented toward capital. In east Germany's present situation, however, assistance should start with improving the capabilities of the work force and the generation of ideas for new products and innovations.

Second, because east Germany is being integrated into west Germany's highly developed social security system, east Germans' wages will not be low. With east German wages in 1991 only 20 percent lower than Japan's and equal to one-third of its GDP per worker, it will not become a low-wage region competing with any of the Southeast Asian countries.[60] In 1992, average wage unit costs rose to more than 200 percent of the west German level, by no means low itself.

Absorption and Transfer Problems

Investment in east Germany was DM 72.4 billion in 1991 and is expected to be DM 75 billion in 1992. This amounts to 22 percent and 23.7 percent, respectively, of gross internal demand.[61] From the macroeconomic perspective, this does not yet seem likely to cause noticeable absorption problems. Construction, however, is already showing strains as the high prices and increased demand for foreign workers (mostly from Poland and Czechoslovakia) indicate. Although east Germany is far from being at full employment and full productivity, regional and sectoral bottlenecks (price increases, for example) are already marked. The difficulties are attenuated by the near doubling of east German imports to 63 percent of 1992 GNP, though imports also require considerable east German complementary activities, such as highway expansion and improvements in rail transportation.

In the present context, however, the macroeconomic perspective is not the most relevant. Bottlenecks were experienced in such areas as, for example, the telecommunications system.[62] Some difficulties, in particular the problem of making regional telephone connections, especially with west Germany, have been overcome. Although there is still

31

a backlog in the demand for local lines, adding up to 600,000 new connections in 1992 in the new Länder will all but satisfy this, giving east Germany the same telephone density as west Germany and an even more advanced technical base within the next ten years.[63] Other problems, more difficult to overcome quickly, include the outmoded railroads and highways as well as limited and still inefficient administrative capabilities, which are particularly painful. Despite the temporary transfer of more than 20,000 west German civil servants to local federal offices, the five new federal and Länder administrations, and the more than 10,000 municipalities, this lack of expertise cannot be offset quickly.

An increase in absorption will require considerable time because of inadequate machinery and the limited capacity of the supply and distribution networks (even when the efficiencies of foreign suppliers are taken into account). More important is the shortage of skilled labor, especially in construction and management. These weaknesses would be alleviated by greater mobility among regions and jobs within Germany, but given the low mobility of the former GDR labor force and the declared goal of having these workers stay in east Germany, the short-term prospects are not bright.[64]

Skilled workers who are mobile will be attracted to west Germany anyway. In 1990, 391,000 east German citizens migrated and 81,000 commuted from east to west Germany; 600,000 migrants and 780,000 commuters are expected in 1993.[65] The potential number of migrants and commuters, however, is difficult to estimate. It depends on the socio-economic developments in east and west Germany, the job opportunities, and the cost of commuting or migrating. Based on 1989 eastern district employment figures, about 3.7 million people, or 45 percent of all permanently employed persons, live in an eighty-kilometer belt along the former intra-German border and around west Berlin (figure 3).[66]

East German officials and employers are ambivalent about labor moving to the west. Mobility does improve income and relieves unemployment in the east, but it is also the third exodus from the region in recent history (after those preceding and following World War II), once more depriving the region of much of its talent just when it is needed most.[67] By the end of 1992, the labor force gainfully employed in the east shrank from 8.5 million to about 5.4 million.

Quickly improving the infrastructure's absorptive capacity requires setting priorities that correspond to the expected future sectoral and

Figure 3. The New FRG and East-West Commuting

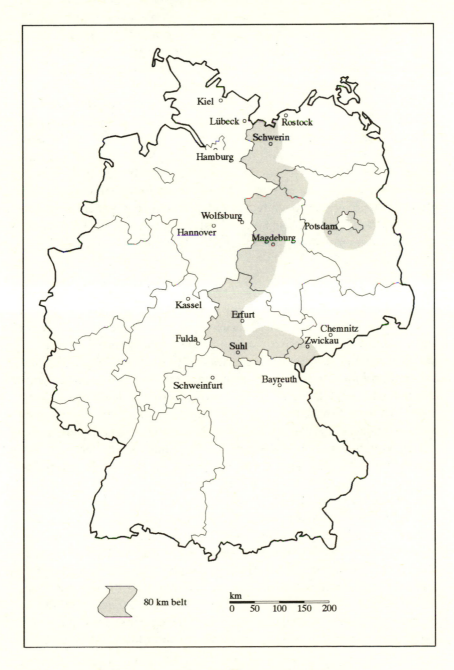

regional structure of the economy. New production requirements and the need for rapid infrastructure improvement would appear to preclude a rail-oriented system. A system relying primarily on roads seems indicated, but that will require long-term planning.[68] Repair and modernization of the infrastructure may proceed along a J-curve—perhaps a general symbol of the process of catching up—where a temporary reduction in capacity precedes any improvement.

The transfer problem has resulted from the large west German transfers on one hand and the strong preferences of the east Germans for west German and foreign products on the other. By 1991, real income per capita had risen one-third higher than its 1989 level. As a consequence, after the MESU, east German production of consumer goods, particularly foodstuffs, suffered declines of up to 60 percent, but it is gradually recovering. So while the transfers immensely increased consumer welfare in east Germany, and sales and jobs in west Germany, they caused many job losses (and thereby additional transfers).

Incomes: Politically Determined or Market Led?

The east German economy, accustomed to balanced development and now uniformly depressed, will come to be characterized by increasing regional and sectoral differentiation. For example, the textile and shipbuilding industries, heavily protected from international competition in the former GDR, will play a significant role in this process. They now have been exposed to competition and are experiencing declines already endured by these industries in west Germany. There is no reason why industries in the two parts of Germany should perfom very differently in the long term, although it is not yet possible to determine exactly who will be winners or losers. One probable winner is east German agriculture, where the traditionally large farms allow much more efficient operation than do west German farms.[69]

Nevertheless, income differences between east and west as well as disparities in health care, education, and housing will not disappear quickly. Limited time and limited physical and financial resources will prevent the government from further alleviating these differences soon. A simple calculation shows that west Germany cannot continue to increase transfers to equalize income and living conditions in the two parts of Germany. The difference in average monthly wage income per capita in 1992 was about DM 1,000.[70] Additional transfers of DM 95 billion a year would be needed to close this gap, an increase of DM 3,000 per west German employee over the DM 5,400 per employee already transferred.

Settlements in early 1991 were intended to establish parity between east and west German wages in the next few years, but they cannot simultaneously stabilize the level of employment. The faster the pace of wage equalization without accompanying improvements in productivity, the greater the number of jobs lost. Because hope for the grand quick fix has vanished, expectations must be adjusted to a much longer time frame.

According to present settlements, equality of negotiated wages is to be reached by 1994, while progress toward shorter work weeks, longer vacations, and other benefits will not take place before 1997. The disparity in number of hours worked in east and west Germany and the fringe benefits available complicate comparisons of hourly wage rates. In 1991, for example, negotiated wages in the east German (Saxonian) metal industry were 63 percent of the west German (Bavarian) level when calculated on a monthly basis, but the effective hourly rate in the east was only 40 percent of that in the west (52 percent in 1992).[71]

Making up for differences in income is certainly a main goal of east German wage policy. Wages in market economies, however, are influenced by many factors, and one generally valid wage theory does not exist. In the present situation, the effects of wages on income seem to be of less importance than those effects more directly related to the vitalization of the east German economy, such as the employment, incentive, or allocative effects of wage settlements. Although in the long run these effects point in the same direction, in the short run and under present conditions the income effects conflict with the employment and incentive functions of wages.

Because the former GDR had a fairly uniform wage and salary structure, to bring it into parity with the greatly differentiated west German structure requires considerable change. Assuming an average growth of 6 percent a year in west Germany and parity of eastern and western wages in five years, the salaries of the highest ranking eastern employees would have to increase by 40 percent a year and wages overall would have to increase by 30 percent (based on 1989 levels). As for sectoral wage differences, annual increases would have to amount to more than 60 percent in some cases.[72] (Interestingly, since 1991 sectoral wage differentiation seems to have decreased.)[73] The great stress such differentiation would cause in a society that considered itself egalitarian cannot be overemphasized. There are wage disparities between workers in the same occupations in the same city (west Berlin) because of different residences, as well as between the unemployed and employed.[74]

In talking about nominal wage rates one should consider that the cost of living in the new Länder is rising faster than in the west because the GDR subsidies for rents, utilities, and public transport are being gradually reduced or have been eliminated. Thus, in contrast to a more favorable situation in 1990, real income of all income-earning workers and employees has shrunk, except for a small group of better-paid employees.

Heavy wage subsidization would also be needed to reduce the conflict between the income and employment effects of wages.[75] Two aspects of wage policy should be emphasized.[76] First, any large-scale subsidization scheme would encounter greater technical difficulties in setting wages now than it would have had, for instance, in mid-1990. The subsidizing agency would have to decide on the sectoral, regional, and occupational wage spread necessary to meet future labor market requirements. Second, the east German employment problem primarily concerns its difficulties in making high-quality products that compete on the world market, not wage policy.[77]

In the short term, east German unemployment and poor competitiveness are partly the result of former production links and a rather inelastic price demand in Eastern Europe and the Soviet Union. The 1991 wage round was another impediment to reviving the east German economy. Moreover, because unemployment benefits are linked to current wages, the wage round has led to further increases in the transfers for unemployment assistance—DM 9.5 billion and DM 17 billion in 1991 and 1992, respectively.

All in all, there is no pat answer to the conflicting demands east German wage policy must accommodate under present conditions. The productivity-oriented wage policy long favored in west Germany was basically intended to reduce inflationary pressure in a full-employment economy by stabilizing income distribution. When unemployment rapidly increased in the 1970s, this approach to wage policy came under attack and was smoothly modified. This formula is inappropriate for east Germany, however, not only because of its high unemployment and the impossibility of isolating east and west German labor markets, but also because past and recent modest productivity gains in east Germany are due mostly to large-scale layoffs and not as yet to long-term gains in productivity.[78]

Structural Considerations

For the time being, east Germany will be confronted with a considerable lag behind west Germany in gross and net income as well as with increasing unemployment. Given the conversion rate of the GDR mark, the high exchange rate of the deutsche mark, high interest rates, and high wage settlements, sectoral and regional structures will have increasing unemployment and continuing worker migration.

When the east German outlook is considered against the *Wirtschaftswunder*, the disadvantage posed by the absence of an exchange rate lever in east Germany can hardly be overstated. Much of the FRG's economic policy in the 1950s and 1960s was driven by the fear of a revaluation of the deutsche mark against the dollar. The few revaluations of the German currency under the Bretton Woods system were only made reluctantly and later proved too small. The prevailing attitude was called the "Abs syndrome," for Hermann Josef Abs, the spokesman for the Deutsche Bank, whose familiar refrain was "Chancellor, chancellor, hands off the deutsche mark! All our hopes for reconstructing the economy and integrating it into the west and for economic growth depend on our low exchange rate against the dollar" (and thus the world economy). That is, the hopes depended on the ability to export and to pay back the debts inherited from the former Reich. There is no doubt that the undervalued deutsche mark was a cornerstone of the quick recovery of the FRG economy, its integration in the world economy, and its subsequent prosperity.

The future sectoral structure of the east German economy is still difficult to predict. Assuming that east German migration and commuting increase no further but west Germany still experiences new growth from an unlimited supply of labor originating in Eastern Europe (the Lewis hypothesis),[79] that east German wages soon reach the high west German levels, and that the capital intensity of the east German economy continues to increase because of generous investment subsidies,[80] the east German industrial structure may begin to approximate west

Germany's, though it may first develop as a kind of extended workbench. Despite all differences, the production structures of both have always showed a marked industrial bias and their demand structures have showed an export bias, though, of course, with different regional orientations. Assuming further that east Germany manages to catch up with west German productivity and income levels in the next ten years, the economy's main sectoral shifts would occur in agriculture (a reduction from 13 percent of GDP in 1986 to about 5 percent) and in the service sector (an increase from 18 percent to 54 percent). The industrial sector would fall from 66 percent to 31 percent of GDP.[81] East Germany's natural resources (lignite) and proximity to Eastern Europe, combined with its traditional trade patterns, might also help conserve elements of the present structure.

This process implies an increasing transfer of west German economic activity to east Germany. However, large-scale shifts of investment, jobs, or sales from west to east cannot yet be detected. West German public investment will grow by 2.0 to 2.5 percent in 1992 and 1993, though this implies a reduction in real terms of more than 4 percent.[82] Business investment in east Germany, which reached DM 45 billion in 1992 (up from DM 26 billion in 1991),[83] is still small compared with total German investment of more than DM 600 billion.[84] Medium-term forecasts, however, are already considering substitution effects. For example, the Institut für Arbeitsmarkt- und Berufsforschung forecast of investment expects only a slight increase of the west German investment ratio to 22.5 percent of GNP.[85] Assuming that this implies a reduction of 1.0 to 1.5 percent of GNP, or DM 25 billion to DM 36 billion, this would not greatly impair west Germany's growth— the study expects a slowdown to 2 percent GNP growth—nor would it meet the needs of east German vitalization.

Solid evidence of such reallocations, despite the massive subsidization of east German investment, is still difficult to detect. Most examples are to be found in the public sector, as in the conflict between Bonn and Berlin over the future site of the capital or between the old and new Länder concerning the locations of the higher courts or federal government agencies. The lack of a shift in economic activity sheds light on some of these difficulties in the public domain of the *Beitrittsgebiet*—the accession territory (as east Germany is legally termed). Its territory is less than half the size of west Germany and its population is only one-fifth that of the new FRG (figure 4). Although

Figure 4. Area and Population of the Länder in the New FRG, 1990

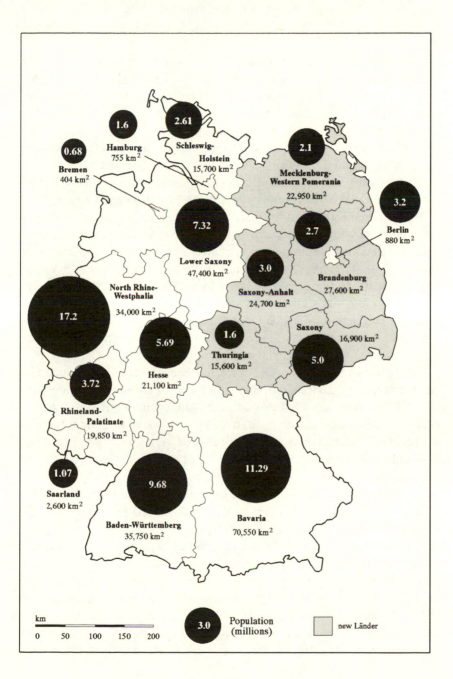

before unification it was seen as an equal partner of the FRG, the fact is that the GDR joined the FRG and not the other way round. Finally, east Germany has far fewer professionals, a gap that will persist in the near term.[86]

Still, on a small scale, relocation of jobs to more competitive east German firms or production units is happening. To the people involved, this is as strongly felt as any large-scale layoffs in the new Länder. The increasingly competitive relationship between east and west Germany is also beginning to be felt in questions concerning sectoral policy, as for instance in the debate over the European Community's concept for east Germany's shipbuilding industry, or when west German hard coal or agricultural subsidies are criticized. (In 1988 these equaled DM 53,591 per employee in the coal industry and DM 24,070 in agriculture.)[87]

East Germany shares with west Germany some industrial proclivities. In 1990 about 40 percent of investment in east Germany was intended to go to manufacturing, a quarter of this to automobile manufacturing. In 1991 these shares may have been even larger.[88] These figures recall the familiar criticism of west Germany—that it is over-industrialized.[89] They also recall another, related structural characteristic the two parts of Germany share: their strong export orientation. This leads some observers to see east Germany's exports to the east as a precondition of its industrial realignment.[90]

Because east German capital stock has been devalued and much has to be scrapped or modernized, there is a huge backlog of investment demand. The extent to which this demand—independent of stabilization fears caused by unmatched fiscal needs of excessive wage increases—will drive up interest rates is difficult to predict. As with fiscal deficits, it could be argued that the amounts involved do not exceed DM 90 billion.[91] Given a world supply of savings of $4,200 billion in 1989, the investment demand should not have too great an effect on interest rates. (In the medium term things may be different—a rather high worldwide capital demand is expected.) However, not only do the various uses of capital and savings and their profitability as seen from the investor's perspective have to be taken into account, but so do their various sources. The interactions involved are complex and probably far from stable enough for sound predictions. Empirical evidence in general, and in the German case in particular, should not rely too much on the equalization effects of the international capital market under present circumstances.[92] If reducing net exports should be only a temporary source of finance, fiscal and monetary policy would be required not only to foster investment in east Germany but also to increase German savings. The 1992 west German private household savings rate was about 13.5 percent of disposable income; an increase to 15 percent would mean an additional DM 25 billion. The number of channels to achieve this are, however, limited: consumption seems not to be very interest elastic, leaving changes in the personal and functional distribution of income as alternative ways to increase savings. From the savings perspective, reducing government deficits becomes therefore too high a priority.

For the stock of labor the demand conditions will remain different. To what extent labor's current perspective will determine the selection of production technologies and products is difficult to judge. Clear investment trends at the sectoral level have not yet been discovered. The most dynamic development has resulted from public investment in physical infrastructure and has been restricted to construction and related industries. Regional development indicates the persistence of present structures, perhaps with the exception of Brandenburg. Growth poles in the classic sense cannot yet be discerned, but remain at the traditional centers of economic activity: Berlin, the capitals of the Länder (Dresden, Erfurt, Magdeburg, Potsdam, and Schwerin), as well as Leipzig, Halle, Rostock, Chemnitz, Jena, Frankfurt an der Oder, and Desau.[93]

Given their large number and urgency, problems in the nonfinancial sector will not be solved without government intervention, and no single policy or measure can address them all. Multiple related measures are called for—on the supply as well as the demand side, the macroeconomic as well as the sectoral and regional levels—and they need time to become effective. Temporary contradictions and offsetting factors will be difficult to overlook. Constraints that have to be adopted in any case are the present relative level of fiscal involvement on one hand and the assurance of all-German growth on the other. However, the recursive nature of fiscal problems should be acknowledged; they cannot be solved independently of other economic difficulties.

The Economic Restructuring of North Rhine–Westphalia

With unification, the problem of vitalizing an entire state-run national economy has become the problem of vitalizing regional economies and coping with an assortment of regional concerns. As mentioned earlier, in the new context in which these problems are to be solved, there is no exchange-rate lever, no common legal and regulatory framework. The influence of the east German region on fiscal and monetary policies is diminished, and its participation in a fiscal federalism is very new. An informative precedent of coping under such conditions is the restructuring of older industrial areas in west Germany.

Aside from federal policies already implemented, fiscal constraints and the FRG's general economic concept greatly restrict additional aid, leaving the new Länder very much on their own to shape their economic policy. For instance, if Brandenburg merged with Berlin to become the biggest of the new Länder, its economic policy agenda might read as follows: to develop Berlin as a metropolitan area with all the functions of a federal capital city; to create and preserve an ample supply of business zones; to plan and implement job-promoting activities; to safeguard those Treuhand enterprises in its territory that go unsold; to promote Eastern trade; and to support the middle class and small enterprises. Except for safeguarding Treuhand enterprises and promoting Eastern trade, such an agenda very much resembles the strategies pursued in comparable west German Länder.

One west German example of economic renovation took place in North Rhine–Westphalia, with its population of 17.5 million citizens (see figure 4). Despite undeniable differences, the renovation bears comparison with the impending transformation in the east German economy with its 16.6 million inhabitants, in particular because of the wholesale transfer of economic policy instruments to the new Länder in 1990 and 1991.

In the late 1950s when the first crisis in the coal industry erupted in the Ruhr region—then the industrial center of West Germany—the Land of North Rhine–Westphalia found itself in economic straits similar to those of the new German Länder today, though not nearly so critical in scale or urgency. The principal requirements were to streamline its existing industrial structure and add new industries. As in the former GDR, unpolluted industrial sites were scarce, and although the skill level of the labor force was decidedly high by international standards, it was geared entirely to traditional and increasingly obsolescent technologies. The scientific, technical, and educational infrastructure was weak.[94] Finally, the environment was heavily damaged.

North Rhine–Westphalia resolved to confront its difficulties aggressively. It attempted to improve its flexibility. As part of a comprehensive plan, education and the infrastructure were addressed first. Additional universities were established and new research centers created. In a second stage a network of vocational and professional training facilities (with 20,000 training places in interfirm vocational education training centers) was created. The facilities sparked technological and innovative initiatives throughout the region. As a result, North Rhine–Westphalia today possesses the best-developed network of universities and research centers in Germany.

Many special programs also encouraged structural change. They were based on the belief that a regional upswing and restructuring designed to safeguard future prosperity could only be set in motion from within: they had to be triggered by the region itself and activate regional development potential. Technology centers established through local endeavors helped transform scientific findings into innovative products and processes. Such centers proved extremely useful, particularly for small- and medium-sized enterprises involved in pioneering ventures.

These efforts have proved successful. The loss of jobs in coal and steel has been offset by the creation of new jobs in more innovative, future-oriented industries and in the service sector, particularly in production-related, research, and market-oriented services. Substantial headway has also been achieved in manufacturing capital goods, primarily in small- and medium-sized businesses that specialize in machine tools and environmental technologies. This sector is now the biggest employer among the major industries in North Rhine–Westphalia and in the Ruhr area. The economic structure of the region now differs radically from what it was in the 1960s.[95]

Of course, no mere copy of North Rhine–Westphalia's strategy will enable the new Länder to attack their problems. The problems are much too large and the time available far too short. Restructuring took more than twenty-five years in North Rhine–Westphalia and has still not been completed. It has required expenditures of several hundred billion deutsche marks; and its success has been very much linked to growth in the rest of the FRG and the EC. Nevertheless, the approach chosen in North Rhine–Westphalia does suggest possible solutions for the problems of east Germany.

The Future of Federal Principles in Germany and Europe

Changes in the European economy to which Germany, and thus the new Länder, now belong create the conditions for structural policy and influence the size of the demands made on the EC member countries' regions or states and the performance expected.

Europe is headed toward creating a European Union, starting with the single market and culminating in an Economic and Monetary Union, with its implied "Europe of regions" (figure 5). European integration has already imposed limits on the nation-state's sovereign capacity to control employment in its regions and sectors. The nation-state's traditional means of creating or preserving jobs—quantitative restrictions, customs tariffs, exchange rates, direct awards of public orders for buildings and procurement, nontariff barriers—will all be abolished in the EC countries. In this way the nation-state will continue to lay down its economic weapons in favor of European liberalization, deregulation, and harmonization. Subsidies and mergers that distort competition will be banned. This amounts to a politically motivated abolition of the frontiers of the nation-state. Market forces are expected to ensure the efficient allocation of resources unobstructed by national or regional frontiers. Interventionist policies, if still possible at all, must be approved by the EC Commission or the Council of Ministers.

New Locational Patterns

The new organization of allocation, however, requires a new role for governments to ensure that market results are also acceptable in terms of social benefits and goals. With respect to the new Länder, this presupposes that the democratic, constitutional, and social body politic and its infrastructure be developed and put in good order. Thus a comprehensive approach must be a key component of structural policy from the outset. Creating stable laws governing capital investment must likewise receive high priority. Restricted compensation must generally prevail over return of assets. But even at the end of 1992, no draft compensation act was at hand.

This brings us to another trend affecting regional economic development: location. Several industrial revolutions and increasing prosperity have led to spectacular changes in the determinants of economic and industrial locations. Locations of industrial plants today—apart, perhaps, from those in primary production and basic goods—are no longer exclusively determined by favorable geography, geology, and demography. Good transportation links and reliable energy sources are potentially available everywhere, making the other determinants less important.

44

Figure 5. Area and Population of the New FRG and the Rest of the European Community, 1990

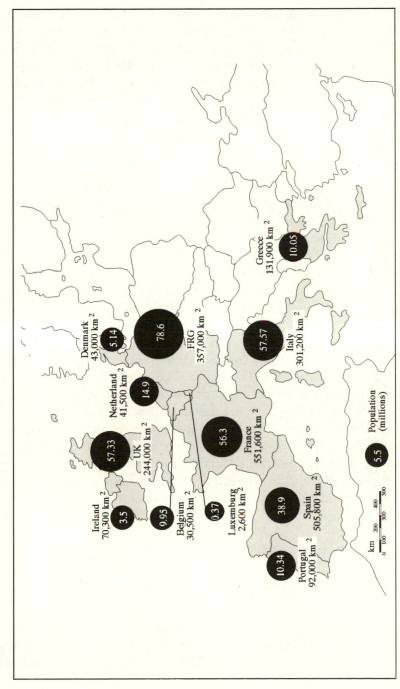

Quite different locational determinants, referred to as soft factors, have emerged. These are a labor force characterized by high standards of schooling, vocational training, university study, and work experience; complementary research, cultural, and leisure facilities; a high quality of urban and regional development; and generally the attractiveness of the region, the quality of life it offers, the intellectual atmosphere, and the range of services available.

In present-day industrial and service societies, industrial output and production- and business-related services are complementary. Only in such a complex web of interdependence can the value added that ensures a lasting basis for growth develop. The quality of transportation links, the energy supply, and telecommunications (the so-called hard locational factors) has long been an indispensable precondition for any kind of economic activity. At the same time, soft locational factors owe their existence to a new quality of the state. The state no longer acts in its former capacities as the sovereign rule, the distributor of privilege, and the arbiter of opportunity (via defense orders, textile quotas, or the allocation of other goods and services). Instead, the state, as it is now being defined, tends to act indirectly. It creates a supply-oriented system with the assistance of local participants, to which all those engaged in economic activity can gear their efforts.

The capacity to develop and take advantage of soft locational factors is open to all, not just to those well endowed by geography, geology, and demography, or those that are particularly needy and structurally weak (and thus eligible for government support), as the new Länder tend to be. A new quality comes to the fore with regard to regional policymaking. Every nation-state and its regions and localities now compete with every other, a fact with implications for national organization in the member countries of the European Community, as well as in all the other nations influenced by the European economic area.

Restructuring German Federalism

German unification may affect German federalism with respect to the territorial boundaries of the Länder, a matter that has been pending for more than twenty-five years, and with respect to the relationship between the federal and the Länder governments. These matters are of particular importance because of the European unification process, in which subnational regions such as the Länder will have to carry greater weight.

46

There is no chance of Germany's return to Prussian dominance or the old German Empire or of any general turn to centralist or imperial modes. Prussian hegemony and the empire were but a brief interlude in German history. The federative elements are much more deeply rooted—they can be traced back to the thirteenth century. Although Germany's commitment to federal structure is not disputed, the relative weights of the federal and the Länder governments have changed, at least temporarily, in the course of unification. These weights were originally set under the Financial System Reform of 1969, which tended to favor cooperative federalism with unitarian elements. The reform resulted more in power sharing than in decentralization. Whether this balance will remain is an open question that is currently the subject of constitutional reform under article 5 of the Unification Treaty and article 146 of the German Basic Law.[96]

Germany's unification can be viewed as a renewed impulse toward centralization, though this runs contrary to the constitutional intentions of the Basic Law and the consensus of the policymakers. It is now primarily up to the federal government to decide whether to support the federative structure and restore the balance between the federal and Länder governments in favor of the Länder or whether to consolidate and strengthen the surge of centralization brought about by unification. One prerequisite to restoring balance is that the federal government leave the Länder governments sufficient room for maneuver in financial matters. Hence, the Länder fiscal compensation arrangements with the central government and among themselves must be reformed. The new Länder are excluded from these arrangements until 1994 (though they fought this exclusion), and the old Länder have attacked the present settlement as being inadequate and unacceptable.[97] So far, however, the federal government appears determined to take advantage of unification to foster certain tendencies toward centralization. One such example is the revision of the Bundesbank's regional structure from eleven state central bank districts (or sixteen including the new Länder) to nine; some observers interpret this action as a precedent for restructuring the Länder themselves.

In the debate over the role of the Länder one must remember that the Basic Law does not guarantee the Länders' number, size, boundaries, or precise duties. Instead, it provides an abstract guarantee of their existence and function: the federation constituted by Länder is to be subdivided into Länder, and they are to have a say in federal legislation.

Restructuring the Länder would be possible only through a very complicated process that would require the concerted effort of the federal government.

In view of Europe's future course, it certainly appears to make sense to create Länder that are capable of performing well over the long term and able to hold their own in any "Europe of regions." The federal government thus ought to take the lead in creating economically viable bases in its constituent states. It must avoid top-heavy, power-oriented centralization that fosters permanent dependence on fiscal transfers from the central government or other Länder. Just as the failure of the centrally planned economies has demonstrated the folly of supposing that all major European governmental functions could be performed by European Community institutions, so only a decentralized German system, structured along federative lines and subscribing to the principle of subsidiarity, can duly cope with both regional and national tasks and concerns.

What is essential is to foster the surge of development potential in the regions themselves. Neither the single market nor the European Union constitutes an event taking place only in Brussels. It is in its regions that Europe lives, and this reality must be accommodated in the debate on the new Germany, along with the recognition that the new Germany is conceivable only in a new Europe.

The Role of Economists: Reluctant and Late

Despite the importance and difficulty of economic issues brought up by unification, economists inside and outside government have done little to shape economic policies. Although deplorable, this development is not unusual in a fundamentally new situation—it was much the same for the FRG's economic decisionmaking during the late 1940s and early 1950s.[98] A remarkable difference this time, however, was the limited participation of several federal ministers of economic affairs, Helmut Haussmann and Jürgen Möllemann, and of the ministry itself. The economic and fiscal difficulties of unification appeared to be only two of a host of matters that had to be settled during the twelve weeks of negotiations leading to the MESU. The negotiation of this first state treaty was led by the Federal Ministry of Finance, aided by the Bundesbank and the Federal Ministry of the Interior. The negotiation of the second state treaty, the Unification Treaty, was led by the Federal

Ministry of the Interior. The Federal Ministry of Economic Affairs showed little interest. Thus economic questions received far less attention than they attracted soon after unification.[99]

Given the apparent lack of demand for economic advice, academicians, stunned anyway by the speed of events, evidently saw no great need to interfere. Nevertheless, economists participated, to varying degrees, in the many stages of unification and the ensuing debates.[100] Discussion peaked when the decisions on the MESU and the conversion rate were made. Most economists were skeptical about the benefits of immediate conversion and the one-to-one rate: the new Germany would not be an optimum currency area with respect to economic growth or price stability, and the conversion rate had little relation to east German productivity (even at its greatly overestimated level) or to the previous artificial exchange rate.

The most prominent voice on economic matters belonged to the Council of Economic Experts (Sachverständigenrat), which on February 8, 1990, urged the chancellor to initiate a five-year gradual rapprochement during which the two economies would remain independent, linked by a fixed exchange rate and restrictions on migration. The west German government, however, decided to subordinate economic considerations to the political imperative of unification.[101] Given the right of all Germans to choose their domiciles and the huge differences in incomes and living conditions between east and west Germans, it would have been impossible to maintain two German currency areas. At the same time that MESU served as an irrepressible engine propelling both sides toward unification, the union and the resulting fiscal transfers (and to some extent the necessary private investment flows from west to east Germany) could only be accepted by west Germans because political unity was imminent. It is of little comfort to economists that economic logic and laws are now getting their revenge for having been pushed aside by political will.

With the benefit of hindsight one knows that the conversion rate was set much too high. The evaluation of east German competitiveness made after the fall of the Berlin Wall and before the MESU became effective on July 1 turned out to be severely wrong and has had to be repeatedly revised. The MESU and the tremendous appreciation of the currency proved to have an effect on the east German economy that was far more sweeping than expected. In particular, east Germany was far less attractive to west German and foreign investors than had been expected. But the widespread expectation or fear that east Germans would plunder their generously converted savings accounts also failed to materialize.

Despite the importance of the conversion decision, in the long run a more accurate picture of the GDR economy would hardly have made much difference, either for the decision itself or for the future of the east German economy, given the political will to unify and the Basic Law, which decreed equal citizenship for east Germans. Even the amount of fiscal aid might not in the end have been very different: a less favorable conversion rate would have meant even greater direct transfers via unemployment relief, social security pensions, and the Treuhandanstalt to help fulfill east Germans' expectations of quickly improving their standard of living. What should have been different is the strategy to revive the economy: the choice to emphasize high-technology development should have been rethought, though it is difficult to imagine how modifications of the FRG economic policy would have been possible in 1990.

To some extent, various diagnostic and prognostic failures explain the misjudgment. For example, after the signing of the MESU, German economic integration devalued the locational advantages of the former GDR with respect to inter-German production and trade, and trade with Eastern Europe. Thus the need to invest in east Germany was undercut. Other explanations for error include the largely unsettled property question, administrative inefficiencies and weaknesses, the collapse of trade among former Communist bloc nations, and the increasing crowds of migrants and commuters that reduced the west German shortage of labor in some sectors. In short, the overestimation of GDR productivity was followed by an underestimation of the difficulty of improving it quickly. A further misjudgment, though partly a consequence of the first error, was the estimate of the fiscal costs of unification. In July 1990 it stood at DM 22 billion for the second half of 1990; now it is estimated that unification will cost up to DM 180 billion a year for the next few years, and the exponential growth of transfer payments may not yet have ceased.

Of greater seriousness than these diagnostic mistakes was the failure of German economists to respond specifically to the vast and sweeping tasks of reconstruction and vitalization, especially as the prospects for the east German economy became increasingly gloomy. The necessity for a tax increase was west German economists' sole focus; but given the depressed income in east Germany and the limited sources of tax revenue, this question only concerned west Germany.[102]

Subsequent west German forecasts repeatedly postponed the time of the hoped-for turnaround of east German production from late 1990 to 1991, into 1992, and now into 1993. But except for eliminating the obstacles mentioned above, no one raised the alarm for additional measures or policies to spur the east German economy.[103] The Council of Economic Experts suggested concentrating on regional subsidies according to the export-base concept.[104] Others anticipated an investment boom, especially in small enterprises, that would render government concern and intervention unnecessary. Economic advice on coping with expected difficulties, resolving conflicts among the economic tasks, or setting out the relationship between industry and small enterprise was hardly heard before 1991. By that time most of the government's major policy decisions had been made, and management and unions had settled on wages.

One of the few suggestions for action, a proposal for a limited tax haven in east Germany, came from political advisers. This idea was rejected out of fear of large-scale tax evasion by west German businesses, knowledge of the generally minor role taxes would play in the east German economy in the next few years, apprehension about large investment subsidies, and fear that certain tax exemptions would be demanded in west Germany. (The idea of launching new policies in the east that might be later applied to the west gained in popularity as many groups saw a chance to turn the former GDR into a kind of laboratory for ideas that had no chance of being tried in west Germany.)

A number of studies commissioned by the Federal Ministry of Economic Affairs in winter 1990–91 examined whether the FRG's and the European Community's regional, energy, transportation, and competition policies were appropriate or effective for the new Länder.[105] In mid-1991 George Akerlof and others presented their daring proposal for general wage subsidies. Later this year Gerlinde and Hans Werner Sinn recommended combining the solutions to the wage and the privatization problems by trading wage moderation against shares of the former GDR's public property for east German savers. No simple, specific solution emerged to deal with labor's rapidly worsening employment situation. On the local and the state level, unemployment was attacked by creating employment assistance agencies (Beschäftigungsgesellschaften) and professional training centers (Qualifizierungsgesellschaften) and relying on older industrial corporations, government, and, temporarily, the Treuhandanstalt as shareholders.[106] But because of both the Unification Treaty and basic political imperatives to achieve parity quickly, policy still gives priority to "the redistributional use of available resources instead of supporting income-generating activities."[107]

Little thought has gone to dealing with the massive expected layoffs in the private sector and in the government sector (in which two out of three jobs were extraneous). In addition, despite the large number of investment subsidies, which have been extended several times, investors' reluctant response has sparked discussion of still more subsidies, leading investors to adopt a wait-and-see attitude. Thus, at least in public, the administration and government are still underestimating the depth, breadth, and cost of the challenge, and they are still muddling through.

Three factors underlie the very restrained participation of economists in making policy. First, despite the general though disputed disclaimer about the "missing theory" and the administration's contact and information privileges, economists only belatedly accepted German unification as a decision based on political principle beyond their field of judgment or competency.[108] And from the incipient stages to the execution of the Unification Treaty, political authorities considered the economic and fiscal implications of unification less important than political implications.[109]

Second, many economists (and even some government ministries) seem to have thought of the problem of vitalizing the east German economy as a simple repetition of the postwar *Wirtschaftswunder*, forgetting that in fact no miracle ever occurred. Instead, events that would have been extremely difficult to forecast took almost everyone by surprise. Still there was faith in the old saying: "Only the impossible can be achieved at one stroke; miracles take a little longer." Neither the disparate conditions nor the time actually needed to produce another *Wirtschaftswunder* was properly taken into account in 1990. In fact, conditions were far less favorable for rapid integration, reconstruction, and vitalization than in 1948. Nevertheless, many saw the government's task as practically accomplished when the MESU (considered the solution to east German stabilization problems) was established and later when unification and the complete adoption of west Germany's system was accomplished. Only a couple of years, the optimists said, and east Germany would catch up because the market economy would immediately trigger a big bang among its enterprises and activities.

Third, economists forbore participation in policymaking because vitalizing the east German economy under the present economic, political, and social conditions is in essence a problem whose nature is holistic, and complex. It is characterized by myriad trade-offs and conflicts: equity or efficiency, short-term or long-term benefits, private or public activities, and, to be sure, east German versus west German interests.[110] Any analysis of the issues must take this interdependence into account, and this requires a generalized mode of reasoning not widespread among contemporary economists.[111] More important, the options remain genuinely political, a reality economists have difficulty accepting. A report by the academic advisory committee of the Federal Ministry of Economic Affairs, notwithstanding its proper description of the various economic and fiscal problems the German economy is facing, conveys this reluctance.[112] Although there has not been much room for economic deliberation at the level of the very principle of unification, there has been plenty of room at the strategic and operational level, room that remains today.

Conclusions

The conclusions of this paper may be summarized as follows.

UNANTICIPATED COMPLEXITY. Germany's political, social, and economic unification has proved much more complex than had been anticipated. Each task arising from unification and integration is by itself difficult to manage: liberalizing, reconstructing, and vitalizing the economy; coping with drastic changes in social preferences (including the increased concern for the environment); solving the questions of property rights. Taken together, the scope of the tasks is greater than the sum of their parts, in particular because of their interdependent yet conflicting natures.

THE ROLE OF POLITICS. From the outset the economics of German unification has been determined politically. The events of unification and the rate of conversion were political decisions. Most of the day-to-day policies of government agencies and the resulting financial needs are determined by legal or administrative regulations or in response to entitlements. On expenditures as well there is little room to maneuver: for instance, there is little room to settle the conflict over whether to use funds for investment or consumption, because consumption is supported by entitlements that are more or less fixed by law. Only in the future, when the new Länder's own income becomes larger and fixed allocations smaller, will flexibility grow and the administrative domination of the process decrease.

THE ROLE OF ECONOMISTS. Given the comprehensive, complex socioeconomics of unification and the constraints faced by the political process in arriving at acceptable policies, economists' lack of participation since the establishment of the MESU is not surprising. Unfortunately, after dismissing economists and their worried counsel, and optimistically deciding that political decisions were the politically and historically favored road to unity, politicians may have concluded that the laws of economics could be brushed aside. Economists inside the government and outside may err. They may give unwelcome advice. But economics cannot be outlawed by political wishful thinking. The political establishment must accommodate economic realities.

The role of economists remains marginal. Much of their study has concentrated on questions for which politically motivated answers have already been reached—the conversion rate or the macroeconomic and international repercussions of Germany's temporarily unavoidable budget deficits. The crucial issues of how to reconstruct and vitalize the economy—the infrastructure needed, the microeconomics of recreating an export base, the transfer of technology and skills—have received much less attention. The introduction of market institutions and regulations are necessary elements in reconstruction, but taken by themselves they are not sufficient to bring about prosperity in a few years.

For too long, economists have ignored important general questions. How can east Germany's old industrial structure be retooled quickly to render it competitive in the highly specialized German, European, and world market? How can Germany regenerate or create anew the base of income or high value added mandatory for the sustained economic and social survival of each region? Should east Germany strive to replicate west Germany's economic and industrial structure, or should it be an extended workshop of the west at least for a time? Considering the trade balance, exchange rates, and mutual prosperity, what would be the consequences of different economic structures for Germany's future role in the European or the world economy? At a more basic level, on such matters of immediate relevance as the formulation of regional or transport policy, or the timely elimination of various hindrances and bottlenecks, economists have had little to contribute.

RECOMMENDATIONS. Present economic performance in east Germany is much worse than expected in 1990, but a number of helpful measures and policies should soon bear fruit. Although evaluations of present economic policies do not lend themselves to strong recommendations, three points should be recognized.

First, Germany urgently needs a complete and realistic stocktaking of all government and quasi-government financial obligations and resources existing now and expected in the medium term. Decisions must be made on how these expenditures will be financed—whether through making additional budget cuts, increasing taxes (explicitly or through fiscal drag), or incurring further debt. All options will have to be considered. Decisions on further tax hikes will require an extremely delicate balance among the needs to produce the necessary means to invest, to avoid inflationary pressure, and to ensure equitable distribution, a challenge rarely met even in the most favorable circumstances. Fiscal pressures could be harnessed to attack such longstanding problems in west Germany as how to reduce subsidies or reform the social security system. Whatever the case, the limited additional financial resources that can be mustered in west Germany and absorbed in east Germany require more decisions on priorities than have been made so far. The questions may appear simple and obvious. Up to now they have hardly been asked.

Second, the idea of east Germany's immediate, uniform, and linear catching up should be dismissed, as should the idea that migration to west Germany can or should be stopped. Like all market economies, west Germany has significant regional, sectoral, and occupational differentiation. There is no reason to expect east Germany to be any different. Policy should prepare people for this differentiation as well as for potential conflicts and competition among the various parts of the economy or the society, and, for the time being, between east and west Germany.

Third, given east Germans' high expectations as well as the great cost of catching up, few modes of intervention should be ruled out, especially if they are temporary and if they can be restricted to east Germany. Government intervention in allocation has reached an extent that few in the FRG believed possible three years ago, and it should not be forgotten that west Germany's early years saw much more government intervention, though in retrospect its contribution to the "miracle" is hard to determine. Observers should be aware, however, that there are few well-tested ideas and concepts on which to base more than marginal intervention in the allocative process. Furthermore, if specific intervention is inevitable, it should be limited: in this respect the FRG's record is not all positive.

REVERSING CENTRALIZATION. Unification has been accompanied by a sizable increase in government centralization. For the first years this was probably inevitable. Now the federal government should reverse this tendency. For internal as well as external reasons, the government would be well advised to demonstrate statecraft by strengthening the federal principle. The new Germany will be part of a new Europe, and this will be a Europe of regions in a large European economic area.

A skeptical observer of the political economy of German unification closed his analysis with the question whether the two German states will not only grow *together* but if together they will also *grow*.[113] Our examination of the first two years of Germany's socioeconomic unification has revealed a number of omissions and mistakes made by all parties in the process. Not only have these been costly, but they may also have delayed a rapid advance by east Germany and weakened west German growth potential. However, many of these policies can still be corrected. In fact, given the imperatives of dramatic change in Europe and in the rest of the world, they will have to be.

Appendix
Chronology of the Economics of German Unification

1989

May 2 Hungary begins to dismantle its border fortifications.

August After the influx of hundreds of East German (GDR) citizens, the Federal Republic has to close its embassies in East Berlin (August 8), Budapest (August 14), and Prague (August 23).

September 11 Hungary opens its Austrian borders to East German refugees.

September 30 Bonn and East Berlin agree that the East German citizens who have taken refuge in West German (FRG) embassies in Prague and Warsaw may travel to the West in East German trains passing through GDR territory; 6,300 East German citizens emigrate.

October 3 After the continuous influx into the West German embassies in Prague and Warsaw, thousands more East German citizens are allowed to emigrate.

October 7 Fortieth anniversary of the GDR. USSR President Mikhail Gorbachev in East Berlin.

October 19 Erich Honecker is replaced by Egon Krenz as secretary general of the Socialist Unity party (SED) and as de facto head of state.

November 4 More than a million East German citizens demonstrate in East Berlin for reform. In the following weeks demonstrations occur against the SED in all the larger cities of East Germany.

November 9 The East German Council of Ministers decides to open the borders with West Germany and West Berlin. After the news is made public, thousands of East German citizens stream over the border into West Berlin.

November 12 Hans Modrow replaces Willi Stoph as minister president of the GDR.

November 22 At the "Monday Demonstration" in Leipzig, demonstrators demand reunification for the first time, chanting, "We are one people."

November 28 Chancellor Kohl submits a ten-point plan aimed at overcoming the division of Germany and Europe in which he argues for the development of "confederate structures" between the two German states as a step toward national unity.

December 5 Chancellery senior official Rudolph Seiters and East German Prime Minister Modrow agree on the creation of a foreign exchange fund of DM 2.9 billion, replacing the *Begruessungsgeld* (welcome money) paid hitherto to East German visitors in West Germany. Both sides agree that beginning January 1, 1990, FRG citizens can travel to East Germany without a visa and without exchanging the required minimum amount of money.

December 19–20 Chancellor Kohl and Prime Minister Modrow agree to form a treaty partnership *(Vertragsgemeinschaft)* between the two German states.

1990

January 1 A foreign travel currency fund comes into force, enabling East German citizens to acquire deutsche marks in exchange for GDR marks: DM 100 at an exchange rate of one to one and a further DM 100 at an exchange rate of one to five per calendar year. The FRG pays up to DM 2.15 billion into this fund and East Germany DM 0.75 billion. This replaces the *Begruessungsgeld* of DM 100.

The "law governing the adaptation of support provided to former citizens of the German Democratic Republic and to ethnic Germans from eastern Europe to assist their integration in the Federal Republic" comes into effect. Under it immigrants receive a set integration payment during their first year of unemployment instead of unemployment relief, health insurance payments, or welfare support. When the year ends they receive unemployment insurance according to the individual situation.

January 9 COMECON (Council for Mutual Economic Assistance) meets in Sofia and decides to end all clearing by year's end.

January 12 The GDR constitution is amended to allow private ownership of production facilities and joint ventures with foreigners.

January 28 State parliament elections are held in the Saarland.

February 1 Prime Minister Modrow presents a plan for the stepwise integration of the GDR and FRG. The resulting Germany would be neutral.

February 13 The West German government offers to form a monetary and economic union with the GDR. The GDR's demands for a DM 15 billion solidarity contribution are rejected.

February 26   The first unemployed person is registered in the GDR.

March 1   The Treuhandanstalt is founded to administer all state-owned production units.

March 8   The GDR Council of Ministers allows the operation of autonomous banks in the GDR.

March 18   The first free elections to the GDR parliament are held.

March 20   The FRG's government parties agree to establish a Monetary, Economic, and Social Union (MESU) with the GDR to begin July 1, 1990.

March 30   The FRG parliament passes a supplement to the 1990 federal budget: the budget volume is set at DM 306.9 billion, DM 6.8 billion higher than originally passed. This is, above all, due to the economic and humanitarian emergency aid to East Germany, a total of DM 5.8 billion. Of this sum, DM 4.0 billion is fixed for immediate direct payments to East Germany and DM 1.8 billion for payments to East Germans in the Federal Republic. The net credit loan is estimated at DM 32.9 billion.

April 2   The Bundesbank publishes its proposal for a conversion law to become part of a treaty on monetary, economic, and social union between the FRG and the GDR. On the designated day, all domestic liabilities in the GDR and payments for current transactions (such as wages and pensions) would be converted into deutsche marks at a rate of 2 GDR marks to 1 FRG mark. Wages and pensions would be adjusted to compensate for losses of purchasing power as a result of price reforms before conversion. Preferential treatment would be given to individual bank accounts of up to 2,000 GDR marks a person, which would be converted at an even rate of exchange.

April 4   The federal cabinet enacts tax relief for West German investments in the GDR.

April 12   The GDR government is formed by the Christian Democratic Union (CDU), German Social Union (DSU), Democratic Awakening (DA), Social Democratic party (SPD), and Liberals, headed by Lothar de Maizière.

May 2   The GDR and FRG agree on the exchange rate of the MESU.

May 6   Local parliament elections are held in the GDR.

May 13   State parliament elections are held in Lower Saxony and in North Rhine–Westphalia.

May 18   The first state treaty between the FRG and GDR is signed by Ministers of Finance Theo Waigel and Walter Romberg. Before this the draft contract for the creation of the Monetary, Economic, and Social Union had been approved by the cabinets in Bonn and East Berlin.

The FRG government approves a draft bill establishing the German Unity Fund and a second supplementary budget for 1990.

In the German Unity Fund the FRG commits itself to partially alleviating the deficits in the GDR national budget arising during the transition from a centrally planned economy to a market economy. The costs of financing are to be carried by the federation and Länder (including local communities) via the German Unity Fund. Out of this fund, East Germany is to receive a total of DM 115 billion in the next four and one half years: in 1990, DM 22 billion; 1991, DM 35 billion; 1992, DM 28 billion; 1993, DM 20 billion; 1994, DM 10 billion.

Of the total DM 115 billion, DM 20 billion are to be financed by reductions of the division-related costs and DM 95 billion through credit loans. Federal and Länder governments each contribute half to the annuity (10 percent).

For the fund, federal and Länder governments must defray the following expenditures in the next few years (billions of deutsche marks).

Year	Federal government	Länder
1990	2.0	0.0
1991	5.0	1.0
1992	6.6	2.6
1993	8.8	3.8
1994	9.5	4.5

The federal and Länder governments agree that the current costs of German division, in particular the tax incentives in accordance with the Berlin assistance law and the *Zonenrandförderung* (financial assistance to the regions at the inner-German border) will be abolished within seven years. The FRG government agrees to make detailed proposals of further expenditure cuts.

The second supplementary budget for 1990 is set at DM 311.7 billion, DM 4.8 billion more than the first supplementary budget. DM 2.75 billion goes for starting the financing of pension and unemployment insurance in East Germany. DM 2 billion goes to the German Unity Fund. The higher expenditures are more than offset by a growth-induced surplus of tax receipts, and the net credit loan is reduced to DM 30.9 billion, DM 2 billion lower than originally planned.

June 11 The Deutsche Bundesbank resolves to allow refinancing quotas totaling DM 25 billion to East German credit institutions as of July 1, 1990. The yardstick for the institutions' quota is to be their balance accounts. In East Germany, newly opened branches of West German banks or of foreign banks based in the Federal Republic receive no special refinancing arrangements for their East German transactions.

June 21 The FRG parliament ratifies the "Agreement on the Creation of a Monetary, Economic, and Social Union between the Federal Republic of Germany and the German Democratic Republic" (the First State Treaty). The agreement is scheduled to take effect July 1, 1990. Its terms are as follows.

To achieve monetary union: on July 1, 1990, the deutsche mark is to be introduced as the only legal tender for payment in East Germany. The authorities for issuing currency and banknotes of the Deutsche Bundesbank will be transferred to the monetary region, expanded to include East Germany, according to the Bundesbankgesetz (the Bundesbank Act). Credit and debts in GDR marks at banks in East Germany will be converted to deutsche marks. The general conversion rate will be 2 GDR marks to 1 deutsche mark. An even exchange rate will apply to claims of up to 2,000 GDR marks for persons born after July 1, 1976; up to 4,000 for persons born between July 2, 1931, and July 1, 1976; and up to 6,000 for persons born before July 2, 1931.

Claims of natural or judicial citizens resident outside East Germany that are incurred after December 31, 1989, are subject to an exchange rate of 3 to 1. The exchange rate for claims and liabilities made out in GDR marks and established before July 1, 1990, will be 2 GDR marks for 1 deutsche mark. Wages and salaries set according to wage tariff agreements valid on May 1, 1990, as well as scholarships, pensions, rents, leases, and other regularly occurring payments due after June 30, 1990 (except for installment payments from or into life insurance plans and private retirement insurance plans), will be valued at a rate of 1 to 1.

To carry out the conversion of currency, East Germany will establish an equalization fund. Beginning on July 1, 1990, interest-bearing claims will be allocated to banks and foreign trade operations in East Germany against the equalization fund when capital does not cover obligations because of the currency conversion. The interest rate on these claims is to correspond to the supply rate for money market shares in banks in Frankfurt for a time period corresponding to the interest period (three months, FIBOR).

To achieve economic union: East Germany will create the preconditions for a social market economy, characterized by private property, competition, free prices, and complete freedom of movement of labor, capital, goods, and services. Besides this, East Germany will provide a tax, financial, and budget system compatible with a market economy.

61

East Germany will adopt various economic regulations when the state treaty comes into effect. East Germany commits to

—adjust its economic policy to the goals of the Growth and Stability Bill and obey the principles of free trade as expressed in the GATT;

—take steps to facilitate enterprises' rapid structural adaptation to the new market conditions;

—introduce a price protection and foreign trade protection scheme for the food and agricultural sector within the EC framework of a market-ordered system;

—adopt the FRG's building regulations and regional regulation policy, and ensure that the security and environmental standards that apply for the FRG are observed when issuing licenses for new construction.

The FRG's environmental law will be adopted just as its federative state structure will be. The atomic law will apply immediately upon the national agreement's coming into force. In addition, the principles of competition and social justice—such as the law against restricting competition, the commercial code, the law on private limited companies, and the law on public limited companies—will be introduced.

To achieve social union: Measures are to be enacted to implement labor law regulation appropriate to a social market economy and a comprehensive system of social security.

In East Germany, freedom of association, wage rate autonomy, right to work, working conditions, workers' participation in enterprises, and protection against dismissal will apply in accordance with the law in the FRG.

East Germany will create a pension, health, accident, and unemployment insurance plan in accordance with the FRG regulations. Pension, health, and accident insurance will be handled by a common authority at first; by 1991 it should be part of the FRG system.

East Germany will introduce a social assistance system that corresponds to the FRG's. To overcome financial bottlenecks that will exist after the change, the FRG accords East Germany certain financial allocations: an estimated DM 22 billion for the second half of 1990 and DM 35 billion for 1991. Budget assistance for deferred financing of social insurance is planned; this is set at DM 2.75 billion for 1990 and DM 3 billion for 1991. East Germany's credit authorization is limited to DM 10 billion for 1990 and DM 14 billion for 1991; the FRG's minister of finance can allow the credit limit to be exceeded in case of fundamentally changed conditions.

June 22 The FRG parliament passes the second supplement to the 1990 federal budget: the volume is set at DM 311.8 billion, the net credit loan is estimated at DM 31 billion.

The GDR parliament passes a law to free prices.

July 1 The deutsche mark is introduced into East Germany in accordance with the MESU. The only legal tender is now banknotes issued by the Bundesbank and coins distributed by the FRG. Exceptions to this are East German coins in circulation up to a nominal value of 50 pfennig, which remain legal tender until called in. The conversion of GDR marks to deutsche marks is undertaken exclusively via bank accounts in East Germany. There is no direct exchange of cash. When the State Treaty takes effect, the emergency assistance for refugees from the GDR is to be replaced by the (much lower) integration assistance and pensions according to the foreign pension law.

July 3 The federal government adopts a draft for the federal budget for 1991 and a medium-term financial plan through 1994.

Compared with the debt established in the second supplementary budget of 1990 in the 1991 budget, federal expenditure will rise by 3.9 percent to DM 324 billion. The net credit loan is set at DM 31.3 billion, DM 0.3 billion higher than in the second supplementary budget.

In financial planning through 1994, 3 percent increases in federal expenditures for 1992 to 1994 are expected; the net credit loan is set at DM 24 billion for 1992, at DM 17.5 billion for 1993, and at DM 11.6 billion for 1994.

July 6 The negotiations between the FRG and GDR to establish the legal framework of unification begin. This second State Treaty is to be presented by the end of August.

July 15–16 A meeting in the Caucasus between President Mikhail Gorbachev and Chancellor Helmut Kohl results in the USSR's approval of German unification, with the united Germany a member of the North Atlantic Treaty Organization (NATO).

July 22 The GDR parliament passes its DM 64.2 billion budget with a DM 32 billion deficit (DM 22 billion financed by the German Unity Fund).

August 9 The federal cabinet resolves *not* to submit the 1991 budget and the financial plan through 1994 to parliament. Now that the accession of East Germany in September or October has become likely, the cabinet reasons that the draft budget is in fact only a partial, regional budget that would not contain all revenues and expenditures of the extended national territory and therefore would not be constitutional.

August 23 The GDR parliament decides to join the FRG on October 3, 1990.

August 30 Minister of Finance Waigel announces the third supplement to the 1990 federal budget. DM 20 billion will go to offset the deficits in the East German social insurance scheme. The cabinet is scheduled to vote on the supplement on October 4, the federal parliament on October 24, and the federal council on October 26.

August 31 FRG Minister of the Interior Wolfgang Schäuble and East German Secretary of State Günter Krause sign the Second State Treaty "concerning the restoration of the unity of Germany"—the Unification Treaty. Parliamentary passage is expected by the end of September. The Unification Treaty creates the basis for the merging of the two German states; as of October 3, the national, legal, and economic order of the FRG essentially will apply to East Germany as well.

The Unification Treaty transfers the judicial system of the FRG to the five yet-to-be-established Länder (states) in East Germany; the various exceptions and reservations the treaty allows are limited in time. This applies also to regulations that concern the financial constitution.

—The sales tax yield will be apportioned into an eastern and a western share. In 1991 the east German Länder should receive an average sales tax share of 55 percent of the average share of an inhabitant of the FRG. This share should rise to 70 percent by 1994, and from 1995 on it should be the same as in west Germany.

Special measures to stimulate the east German economy include:

—DM 10 billion for loans with subsidized interest rates for local community investments, which will reduce the interest rate up to 10 percent over ten years.

—DM 10 billion for preferred loans to modernize housing, with a maximum amount of DM 10,000 per applicant.

—A 23 percent investment subsidy according to the framework of the west German system of regional assistance, whose expected costs of DM 3 billion a year are to be met by the federal government and the new Länder.

—Up to 85 percent of the money from the German Unity Fund will be allocated to east German Länder; the remaining 15 percent will be allocated to the federation to fulfill national tasks in east Germany.

September 10 The FRG and the USSR agree that the FRG will contribute DM 12 billion for the USSR's troop withdrawal.

September 20 The FRG and GDR parliaments ratify the Unification Treaty.

October 3 The East German Länder—Brandenburg, Mecklenburg–Western Pomerania, Saxony, Saxony-Anhalt, and Thuringia—join the FRG in accordance with article 23 of the FRG's Basic Law. East and West Berlin form the Länd Berlin. The Basic Law, with the exceptions agreed upon in the Unification Treaty, applies to East Germany.

October 5 The federal cabinet approves the third supplementary budget with an additional DM 20 billion.

October 9 The FRG and the USSR agree on the withdrawal of Soviet troops from the territory of the former GDR. The FRG will give DM 12 billion to the USSR for relocation expenses. DM 7.8 billion will go to finance a housing program for returning soldiers in 1991 and 1992; DM 1 billion will defray the costs of stationing the troops in 1990 and 1991. DM 1 billion will help relocate troops, and DM 0.2 billion will help with education and retraining.

October 14 The first state parliament elections are held in the new Länder.

October 25 The FRG parliament approves the third supplementary budget. Besides the changes for the west German territory, the budget includes the budget of the former GDR from July 22, 1990. The net deficit is DM 25 billion higher than previously planned because of lower revenues and higher expenditures in east Germany.

November 1 The Bundesbank raises the Lombard rate from 8 percent to 8.5 percent effective November 2.

November 14 The federal government announces that it will limit government spending from 1991 to 1994 to increases of no more than 2 percent a year to limit the net deficit in 1991 to DM 70 billion and lower it by 1994 to DM 30 billion. The necessary reallocations are to be DM 35 billion in 1991 and DM 70 billion in 1994.

December 2 The first united German election to the federal parliament is held.

December 13 The Bundesbank announces that it will expand the money supply M3 in 1991 by 4 to 6 percent.

1991

January 1 Old age pensions in east Germany are increased by 15 percent.

January 10 The government provides details on the DM 35 billion deficit reduction scheduled for 1991. Revenues are to be increased by raising various contributions (DM 20.3 billion), privatizing government holdings (DM 0.5 billion), and by various savings (DM 14.2 billion).

The unemployment insurance contribution rate is to increase by 1.5 percent. The contribution rate to the old age pension fund will be lowered by 1 percent. The expected net revenues of these measures are DM 18.3 billion. A special surcharge of the federal post office in 1991–94 is expected to yield DM 2 billion each year and privatization DM 0.5 billion.

Defense expenditures are to be reduced by DM 7.6 billion, tax privileges for Berlin and the former intra-German border regions are to be cut by DM

1.5 billion. The expenditures of the Bundesanstalt für Arbeit (Federal Employment Office) are to be reduced by DM 2.3 billion and fiscal aid by DM 1 billion. Postponing government investments will cut DM 2.3 billion.

January 20   State parliament elections are held in Hesse.

January 31   The Bundesbank raises the discount rate from 6 percent to 6.5 percent and the Lombard rate from 8.5 percent to 9 percent effective February 1.

February 20   The federal government agrees on the 1991 budget with total expenditures of DM 399.7 billion and a net deficit of DM 69.5 billion. According to financial planning through 1994, expenditures in 1992 are to be limited to a 0.8 percent increase and in 1993 and 1994 to 2.2 percent. Net credits are to be restricted to DM 49.4 billion in 1992, DM 40.6 billion in 1993, and DM 30.9 billion in 1994.

February 28   At a conference between Länder ministers and Chancellor Kohl, the federal government resolves to improve the financial situation in eastern Germany with the allocation of approximately DM 22 billion.

—The federal government grants the new Länder additional aid of DM 5 billion for investment in cities, counties, and communities. These funds are to be distributed according to population.

—The federal government renounces its portion of the German Unity Fund and offers an additional DM 7 billion to the new Länder to promote investment and employment.

—Instead of the former step-by-step plan in the Unification Treaty, the new Länder will as of January 1, 1991, benefit from the revenue tax in proportion to their respective populations.

March 8   The federal government creates the Gemeinschaftswerk Aufschwung Ost (Joint Program Upswing East) by levying a 7.5 surcharge on income and corporate taxes between July 1, 1991, and June 30, 1992, and by permanently increasing taxes on mineral oil products, insurance, and tobacco. Parts of the revenues are to be used to

—improve local infrastructure, in particular to modernize hospitals and homes for the elderly (1991: DM 5 billion);

—speed up vocational training as well as establish new enterprises (1991: DM 2.5 billion; 1992: DM 3 billion);

—speed the improvement of the transportation infrastructure (1991: DM 1.4 billion; 1992 DM 4.2 billion);

—modernize housing and city and village renovation (1991, 1992: DM 1.1 billion);

—extend the deadlines for increased investment subsidies to the end of 1991–92 and allow them to be combined with special depreciation (1991:

DM 0.4 billion; 1992: DM 0.65 billion);

—concentrate regional assistance for job creation programs in depressed areas (1991, 1992: DM 0.6 billion);

—assist the adjustment process in the shipbuilding industry (1991: DM 0.13 billion; 1992: DM 0.4 billion);

—provide emergency assistance for the environment (1991, 1992: DM 0.4 billion);

—modernize university buildings and student housing (1991, 1992: DM 0.2 billion);

—renovate federal buildings (1991: DM 0.27 billion; 1992: DM 0.05 billion).

March 20 The federal parliament passes the Gesetz über Beseitigung von Hemmnissen bei der Privatisierung von Unternehmen und zur Förderung von Investitionen (Act Governing Removal of Impediments in the Privatization of Enterprises and the Promotion of Investment). The bill is mainly intended to provide the legal provisions for carrying out investments when restitution claims are not yet decided on. In addition, the revision of the Umweltrahmengesetz (Framework Law on Environmental Protection) frees investors from covering environmental damages caused before July 1, 1990.

April 18 The Zentralbankrat (Central Bank Council) of the Bundesbank reports for 1990 a net profit of DM 9,118 billion, of which DM 8,265 billion is transferred to the federal government.

April 21 State parliament elections are held in Rhineland-Palatinate.

May 14 The federal parliament extends the special regulations for payments to short-term workers in the new Länder beyond December 31, 1991. The special regulations for job-creating activities in these states are extended beyond 1992. The age limit for certain pension claims is reduced from 57 years to 55 years.

June 2 State parliament elections are held in Hamburg.

June 7 The federal parliament approves the budget for 1992, which shows an 8 percent increase over the 1990 budget and its three supplements. Proposed net expenditures for 1991 amount to DM 66.4 billion.

June 13 The Bundesbank adjusts the conditions for refinancing by east German banks to west German regulations. East German rediscount conditions are reduced by DM 6 billion; other adjustments lower its potential for credit further.

June 17 The federal government plans to increase the VAT in 1993 and to lower corporate taxes.

July 1 Old age pensions in east Germany are increased by 15 percent. Laws increasing taxes on income, gasoline, insurance, and tobacco come into effect. Their estimated revenues for 1991 are DM 17.4 billion, and for 1992, DM 26.8 billion. In east Germany various taxes are reduced (special depreciation rates, income tax), with an estimated volume in 1991 of DM 2.5 billion, and in 1992 of DM 3.4 billion.

July 10 The federal government agrees on the 1992 federal budget and on a financial plan through 1995. Expenditures are expected to rise by 3 percent as compared to the 1991 budget plan, amounting to DM 422.6 billion. The net deficit will shrink by DM 15.2 billion. In 1993 expenditures are expected to increase by 1.4 percent and in 1994 and 1995 by 2.4 percent. Net credits are to be reduced to DM 64 billion in 1993, DM 30.2 billion in 1994, and DM 25.1 billion in 1995.

July 11 The Bundesbank decides to decrease the planned growth of the money supply (M3) from the fourth quarter of 1991 to the first quarter of 1992 by 1 percentage point, which means a 3 to 5 percent increase. The bank sees the reductions as necessary consequences of portfolio adjustment and price increases in the new Länder.

August 15 The Bundesbank raises the discount rate from 6.5 percent to 7.5 percent and the Lombard rate from 9 percent to 9.5 percent effective August 16.

September 2 The federal government agrees on a draft bill to relieve taxes for families and companies by 1992. It will be offset by an increase of the VAT from 14 to 15 percent and by reducing tax exemptions. The federal government decides to repeal the structural aid for the Länder of DM 2.45 billion by 1992 and to increase its contribution to the German Unity Fund by a corresponding amount through 1994. In addition, the federal government will increase its contribution by DM 3.45 billion in 1992 and in 1993 and 1994 by DM 1 billion to improve the fiscal situations of the new Länder.

October 17 The federal government decides on a second budget for 1991 to meet the additional DM 5 billion expenditures for unemployment encountered by the Bundesanstalt für Arbeit in 1992 financed mainly by expenditure savings in 1991.

November 12 The coalition decides to introduce a 25 percent tax on interest income by 1993. Exemptions for savings are increased from DM 600 to 6,000 and for married couples from DM 1,200 to DM 12,000.

November 29 The federal parliament agrees on a budget for 1992 that will top 1991 spending by 2.9 percent. Planned expenditures amount to DM 422.1 billion, with a net deficit of DM 45.3 billion.

The Bundesrat rejects the tax reform law of 1992 and the Struktur-hilfeänderungsgesetz (Structural Assistance Amendment Law).

December 5 The Bundesbank announces its money supply goal: M3 will grow by 3.5 to 5 percent during the fourth quarter of 1991 and first quarter of 1992.

December 10 An arbitration committee is unable to reconcile the federal parliament and the Bundesrat in their conflict over the 1992 tax reform bill.

December 11 The federal government accords the Treuhandanstalt a maximum credit limit of DM 30 billion for 1992–94, but under certain conditions this may be extended by DM 8 billion each year.

December 12 The federal government decides to extend transition payments to the elderly in the new Länder by six months, to June 30.

December 19 The Bundesbank increases the discount rate from 7.5 percent to 8.0 percent and the Lombard rate from 9.25 to 9.75 percent effective December 20.

1992

January 1 The FRG pension law is introduced into the new Länder, and a financial alliance between east and west German old-age pension insurance is created.

February 14 The Bundesrat passes the Steueränderungsgesetz 1992 as well as the Gesetz zur Aufhebung des Strukturhilfegesetzes und zur Aufstockung des Fonds "Deutsche Einheit" (Law to Amend the Structural Assistance Law and Supplement the German Unity Fund) from the compromise version suggested by the arbitrators.

—The annual DM 2.45 billion federal structural aids transferred to the old Länder until now will be used to increase the German Unity Fund and thus to help the new Länder. In addition, the federal share of this fund is increased by DM 3.45 billion to improve the fiscal situation of the east German Länder and local communities.

—Additional federal revenues from the increase of the VAT from 14 to 15 percent (the lower rate for basic goods is left unchanged) in 1993 and 1994 will be used to support the German Unity Fund.

—The Länder will increase their share of VAT revenues from the turnover tax from 35 percent to 37 percent.

—The tax program that eases burdens on families, which began in 1992, will be extended. The *Erstkindergeld* (financial assistance for the firstborn dependent child) is increased from DM 50 to DM 70 a month (an additional

69

expenditure of DM 2.4 billion). Low-income families are to receive an increase from DM 48 to DM 65 per month (an additional expenditure of DM 0.7 billion), and child exemptions are to be raised from DM 3,024 to DM 4,104 (a decrease in revenue in 1992 of DM 3.2 billion and in 1993 of 3.8 billion).

—The tax structure is to be improved in 1993. Among other reforms the net worth tax for companies is to be decreased and also simplified, while the business yields tax will be raised and refined (a decrease in revenue of DM 4.5 billion).

—Additional tax incentives for real estate investment, including exemptions for housing investment loans, will be created over the next four years in accordance with paragraph 10E of the income tax law.

April 5 State parliament elections in Baden-Württemberg and in Schleswig-Holstein are held.

May 13 The federal government decides on a draft supplementary budget for 1992 and the goals for medium-term financial policy.

In the supplementary budget for 1992, expenditures, mainly to finance further investment incentives in the new Länder, are planned to total DM 426 billion, which is DM 3.9 billion more than the previous budget plan. The net deficit is estimated at DM 42.7 billion, a DM 2.6 billion reduction of the previous estimate, resulting from cutbacks and higher tax revenues.

According to the medium-term financial policy:

—Expenditure increases should be limited on average to 2.5 percent a year through 1996.

—The tax moratorium will last until the end of the current legislative term; afterward new financial benefits and the improvement of existing benefits may only be enacted if balanced by similar cutbacks elsewhere.

—Subsidies to the Bundesanstalt für Arbeit are to be terminated through administrative and legal measures.

—The net deficit for 1993 will be fixed at a maximum of DM 40 billion, and at an estimated DM 30 billion in 1994 and DM 25 billion in 1995.

June 3 The federal government decides to extend the 1992 program Gemeinschaftswerk Aufschwung Ost (Joint Program Upswing East).

June 26 The Bundestag passes the second Priority to Investment Bill (March 20, 1991). Existing regulations giving priority to investment if proprietorship of enterprises or land is unclear are united, simplified, and broadened to include single apartments and extended to December 31, 1995.

June 30 The 7.5 percent surcharge on income and corporate taxes, in effect since July 1, 1991, expires.

July 1 The Bundestag decides to increase the basic housing rents in east Germany. The rents are scheduled to rise on January 1, 1993, by at least DM 1.20 per square meter, and at the beginning of 1994 by another DM 0.60. At the beginning of 1995 all housing rents will be free.

July 16 The Bundesbank increases the discount rate from 8.0 percent to 8.75 percent effective July 17.

September 15 The Bundesbank lowers the discount rate from 8.75 percent to 8.25 percent and the Lombard rate from 9.75 percent to 9.5 percent.

October 22 The federal government and the new Länder agree to share the cost of environment damages between these Länder (40 percent) and the Treuhandanstalt (60 percent).

November 27 The Bundestag passes the 1993 federal budget. Expenditures are planned to increase by 2.5 percent to DM 435.6 billion. The net deficit will be DM 43 billion; because of cyclical effects this is DM 5 billion higher than originally planned. The government's contribution to the unemployment insurance system is lowered by DM 2.5 billion. This leads to a 0.2 increase of the contribution rate, which is balanced by a reduction in the pension insurance of the same magnitude.

December 2 The Bundestag decides on an extension (to 1996) and an increase of the subsidies according to the law on investment allowances for east Germany from an average of about 5 percent to 8 percent, and in certain cases up to 20 percent.

December 10 The Bundesbank announces that it will expand M3 in 1993 by 4.5 to 6.5 percent.

Notes

1. This paper focuses on the economic aspects of German unification. For a comprehensive account of the political and social developments in the new Germany see Catherine M. Kelleher, "The New Germany: An Overview," in Paul B. Stares, ed., *The New Germany and the New Europe* (Brookings, 1992), pp. 11–54. For the history of the two Germanies, see, for instance, Henry A. Turner, *The Two Germanies since 1945* (Yale University Press, 1987).

2. For a broader analysis of the east German economy see Rheinisch-Westfälisches Institut für Wirtschaftsforschung, *RWI-Konjunkturberichte*, vol. 43, no. 2 (1992). For a critical evaluation of the various economic indicators in the present east German situation, see Institut für Wirtschaftsforschung, *Ostdeutschland 1992 und 1993: Zerbrechliche Aufwärtsbewegung—Frühjahrsgutachten 1992* (Berlin-Halle, May 1992), pp. 32ff.

3. E. M. Verkade, "Restructuring the East German Economy—Some Model Results," research memorandum 80 (The Hague: Central Planning Bureau, 1991); and Robert J. Barro and Xavier Sala-I-Martin, "Convergence across States and Regions," *Brookings Papers on Economic Activity 1:1991*, pp. 107–58. Their approach is enlarged on and debated in Rudiger Dornbusch and Holger Wolf, "Economic Transition in Eastern Germany," *Brookings Papers on Economic Activity 1: 1992*, pp. 235–61, and the comments and discussion following the paper.

4. Warwick J. McKibbin, "The New Europe and Its Economic Implications for the World Economy" (Brookings and Congressional Budget Office, June 1991).

5. Institut für Wirtschaftsforschung, "Entwicklungstendenzen in Ostdeutschland" (Halle-Berlin, February 1992).

6. Dieter Bogai and others, "Arbeitsplatzförderung statt Lohnersatz," *Werkstattbericht 7* (Nürnberg: Institut für Arbeitsmarkt- und Berufsforschung, May 1992), p. 6. See also Wolfgang Franz, "Aus der Kälte in die Arbeitslosigkeit—Eine Zwischenbilanz der deutschen Arbeitsmarktentwicklung" (Universität Konstanz, September 1992).

7. Compare, for instance, the evaluation of the postwar German economy in Deutsches Institut für Wirtschaftsforschung, *Die deutsche Wirtschaft zwei Jahre nach dem Zusammenbruch: Tatsachen und Probleme* (Berlin: Albert Nauck, 1947).

8. For this section see the sources in note 1 and Erhard Kantzenbach, "Ökonomische Probleme der Deutschen Vereinigung," *Hamburger Jahrbuch für Wirtschafts- und Gesellschaftspolitik*, vol. 35 (1990), pp. 307ff; Jan Priewe and Rudolf Hickel, *Der Preis der Einheit* (Frankfurt am Main: Fischer Taschenbuch Verlag, 1991); and Michael Kreile, "The Political Economy

of the New Germany," in Stares, ed., *New Germany and the New Europe*, pp. 55–92.

9. The net value is arrived at from calculations with the Rheinisch-Westfälisches Institut für Wirtschaftsforschung (RWI) business cycle model for the FRG, ignoring effects of interest rates and concentrating only on the relationship between government expenditures and revenues. The absolute amount, the total expenditure arising from unification, is disputed. Should it include, for instance, the housing program for officers returning home to the former Soviet Union?

10. See the appendix. See also Gerhard Lehmbruch, "Die improvisierte Vereinigung: Die dritte deutsche Republik," *Leviathan*, vol. 15 (1991), pp. 462ff.; Kreile, "Political Economy of the New Germany"; and Ullrich Heilemann, "The Economics of German Unification—A First Appraisal," *Konjunkturpolitik*, vol. 37 (1991), pp. 128ff.

11. Reimut Jochimsen, "Chancen und Herausforderungen der Wirtschafts- und Währungseinheit im vereinigten Deutschland," *Deutsche Bundesbank, Auszüge aus Presseartikeln*, no. 84 (1990), pp. 10ff.

12. Reimut Jochimsen, "The Impact of Monetary Union on the German Economy," *Deutsche Bundesbank, Auszüge aus Presseartikeln*, no. 93 (1990), pp. 11ff.

13. Deutsches Institut für Wirtschaftsforschung, "Quantitative Aspekte einer Reform von Wirtschaft und Finanzen in der DDR," *DIW-Wochenberichte*, no. 17/18 (April 28, 1990); Leslie Lipschitz and Donough McDonald, eds., "German Unification—Economic Issues," IMF occasional paper 75 (Washington: International Monetary Fund, 1990); and Heilemann, "Economics of German Unification."

14. This figure is hard to verify. Macroeconomic as well as sectoral productivity rates (NMP—net material product per worker) have included a considerable inflation component; productivity rates of individual enterprises are difficult to judge because production costs or products often included a number of social services.

15. Routine matters such as filing taxes or taking legal action were completely unknown. Manfred Stolpe, *Schwieriger Aufbruch* (Berlin: Siedler, 1992), pp. 78ff.

16. Even before unification East German goods and services competed poorly in Western export markets, requiring substantial government subsidies and preferential treatment in West Germany and the EC; see Deutsche Bundesbank, *Monatsberichte*, vol. 42 (July 1990), p. 25, note 1. The GDR's expensive exports to the West were clearly intended to acquire convertible currencies to pay its import bill.

17. Deutsche Bundesbank, *Monatsberichte*, vol. 44 (July 1992), pp. 15ff. For a broader picture including investment, see Andras Inotai, *Economic Impact of German Reunification on Central and Eastern Europe* (Budapest: Institute for World Economics, 1991).

18. The basic internal reforms they sought were tackled only twenty years later, spurred by the 1968 student turmoil.

19. For a brief account of this debate from what is now a very ample literature, see Kreile, "Political Economy of the New Germany"; Priewe and Hickel, *Preis der Einheit*, p. 56; Heilemann, "Economics of German Unification, pp. 31ff.; and more generally, the account of the federal minister of the interior in charge of negotiating the Treaty of Unification: Wolfgang Schäuble, *Der Vertrag—Wie ich über die deutsche Einheit verhandelte* (Stuttgart: Deutsche Verlagsanstalt, 1991), pp. 25ff.

20. On this and what follows, see Lehmbruch, "Die improvisierte Vereinigung," pp. 464ff.; and Richard Tilly, "Wirtschaftshistorische Reflektionen über den deutschen Einigungsprozeß im 19. Jahrhundert" (Münster: Universität Münster, 1991).

21. For a broader view summarizing forty years of economic development policy, see Gustav Ranis, "Global Perestroika" (Yale University, 1990). Some striking similarities (as to the promise of prosperity, modernization, regional reevaluation) to the American Reconstruction period exist as well; see Eric Foner, *Reconstruction: America's Unfinished Revolution, 1863–1877* (Harper, 1988), pp. 379ff.

22. Henry C. Wallich, *Mainsprings of German Revival* (Yale University Press, 1955); and Werner Abelshauser, "Die ordnungspolitische Epochenbedeutung der Weltwirtschaftskrise in Deutschland: Ein Beitrag zur Entstehungsgeschichte der Sozialen Marktwirtschaft," in Dietmar Petzina, ed., *Ordnungspolitische Weichenstellungen nach dem Zweiten Weltkrieg*, Schriften des Vereins für Socialpolitik, N.F. 203 (Berlin: Duncker and Humblot, 1991), pp. 11ff.

23. Janos Kornai, *The Road to a Free Economy* (W. W. Norton, 1991); and Heilemann, "Economics of German Unification," pp. 144ff.

24. Schäuble, *Der Vertrag*, p. 251.

25. Stolpe, *Schwieriger Aufbruch*, p. 197.

26. So far, the fiscal costs of the settlement are completely open ended, and there is no information as to how these will be met. In the thirty years after World War II, the FRG spent about DM 130 billion in compensation; see Willi Albers, "Der Lastenausgleich. Rückblick und Beurteilung," *Finanzarchiv*, vol. 47 N.F. (1991), pp. 272ff.

27. Lawrence Weschler, "A Reporter at Large—Shock (Poland)," *New Yorker*, December 10, 1990, p. 97.

28. On this topic see Dietmar Dathe and Bernd Fritzsche, "Ziele, Tätigkeiten und Perspektiven der Treuhandanstalt," RWI papiere 31 (Essen: Rheinisch-Westfälisches Institut für Wirtschaftsforschung, October, 1992); P. Christ and R. Neubauer, *Kolonie im eigenen Land—Die Treuhand* (Berlin: Rowohlt, 1991); Priewe and Hickel, *Der Preis der Einheit*, pp. 164ff.; Sachverständigenrat zur Begutachtung der gesamtwirtschaftlichen Entwicklung, *Auf dem Weg zur wirtschaftlichen Einheit Deutschlands—Jahresgutachten 1990/91* (Stuttgart: Kohlhammer, 1990), pp. 514ff.; Sachverständigenrat zur Begutachtung der gesamtwirtschaftlichen Entwicklung, *Die wirtschaftliche Integration in Deutschland—Jahresgutachten 1991/92* (Stuttgart: Kohlhammer, 1991), pp. 478ff.; Gerlinde Sinn and Hans Werner Sinn, *Kaltstart—*

Volkswirtschaftliche Aspekte der deutschen Vereinigung (Tübingen: Mohr, 1991), pp. 67ff.; Frank Stille, "Zur Politik der Treuhandanstalt—Eine Zwischenbilanz," *DIW-Wochenbericht*, no. 7 (1992); Stolpe, *Schwieriger Aufbruch*, pp. 223ff.; Treuhandanstalt, *Fragen und Antworten zur Privatisierung ehemaligen Volksvermögens in den neuen Bundesländern*, 2d ed. (Berlin: Verlagsgesellschaft Markt und Wirtschaft, 1991), and various monthly reports of the Treuhandanstalt; Wissenschaftlicher Beirat beim Bundesministerium für Wirtschaft, *Probleme der Privatisierung in den neuen Bundesländern* (Bonn: Ministry of Economics, 1991).

29. Institut für Wirtschaftsforschung, *Ostdeutschland 1992 und 1993*, pp. 95ff.

30. See Ernst Helmstädter, "Neue Bundesländer als Industriestandort," *Vitalisierung der ostdeutschen Wirtschaft*, Gespräche der List-Gesellschaft 14 (Baden-Baden: Nomos, 1992), pp. 100ff.

31. For such reasons Manfred Stolpe, Prime Minister of Brandenburg, expects Brandenburg-Berlin to become the Baden-Württemberg or Bavaria (the FRG's growth leader of the 1970s and 1980s) of the next century. Stolpe, *Schwieriger Aufbruch*, p. 207.

32. Barro and Sala-I-Martin, "Convergence across States," pp. 141ff.

33. One of the few attempts to find a solution by combining several problems was made by Sinn and Sinn, *Kaltstart*. They suggested combining privatization and revitalization and first arriving at wage settlements. However, the idea was soon attacked for a number of reasons; see Hermann Ribhegge, "Fehlstart—Der Sozialpakt für den Aufschwung von G. und H.-W. Sinn," *Wirtschaftsdienst*, vol. 72 (1992), p. 152.

34. See Schäuble, *Der Vertrag*, pp. 134ff.

35. Heilemann, "Economics of German Unification," pp. 137ff.

36. Gustav A. Horn, Werner Scheremet, and Rudolf Zwiener, "Domestic and International Macroeconomic Effects of German Economic and Monetary Union," discussion paper 26 (Berlin: DIW); and McKibbin, "New Europe," pp. 14ff.

37. For the effects in Eastern Europe, see Inotai, *Economic Impact of German Reunification*; and Deutsche Bundesbank, *Monatsberichte*, vol. 44 (July 1992), pp. 15ff.

38. Alena Bruestle, Roland Döhrn, and Richard A. Milton, "Die Einbindung der DDR in den Rat für gegenseitige Wirtschaftshilfe," *RWI-Mitteilungen*, vol. 41 (1990), pp. 53ff.

39. Among other reasons for the low estimates are claims on the Treuhandanstalt for debt and interest payments, export guarantees, the costs of undoing vast environmental damage, and claims on the GDR government insurance system.

40. Schäuble, *Der Vertrag*, pp. 184, 187.

41. For instance, there have been various postponements of the scheduled increases of east German housing rents.

42. The national account definition of public investment classifies the building of a school or a public swimming pool as "investment" but salaries

paid to teachers as government "consumption," which is too narrow, particularly in this context.

43. Predemocratic societies often handled the foundation of states in a more generous way. Starting from a government sector share of 5 percent of national income, they managed to raise the share to more than 30 percent. See Gustav Schmoller, "Historische Betrachtung über Staatenbildung und Finanzentwicklung," *Jahrbuch für Gesetzgebung, Verwaltung und Volkswirtschaft im Deutschen Reich*, vol. 33 (1909), p. 8.

44. Wolfgang Kitterer, *Rechtfertigung und Risiken einer Finanzierung der deutschen Einheit durch Staatsverschuldung* (Kiel: Universität Kiel, June 1992), pp. 20ff.

45. In 1988 these exceeded DM 126 billion. HWWA Institut für Wirtschaftsforschung, *Analyse der strukturellen Entwicklung der deutschen Wirtschaft—Strukturbericht 1991* (Hamburg, 1991), pp. 256ff.

46. Bernd Fritzsche and others, "Perspektiven und Optionen der deutschen Finanzpolitik 1991 bis 1994," *Wirtschaftsdienst*, vol. 71 (1991), pp. 21ff.

47. Besides the deficits of the Treuhandanstalt, the federal post office, the federal railway system, and east German railway system, there are the costs for increasing the basic abatement (DM 4.4 billion), repairing damage to the environment, closing down the east German nuclear power stations, help for economic stabilization, additional payments to the EC, and costs resulting from guaranteeing German exports to Eastern Europe.

48. The Community's funds for structural operations, including the cohesion fund, are scheduled to increase from DM 37 billion in 1992 to DM 60 billion (all in 1992 prices), with Germany's part amounting to about DM 18 billion. On this topic and its implications for the EC members see Wolfgang Reinicke, *The New Europe: The Challenge of System Transformation and System Reform* (Brookings, 1992), pp. 79ff.

49. Fritzsche and others, "Perspektiven," pp. 26ff.; McKibbin, "New Europe"; and Deutsches Institut für Wirtschaftsforschung—Wochenbericht, *Quantitative Aspekte einer Reform von Wirtschaft und Finanzen in der DDR* (Berlin, 1990).

50. Rheinisch-Westfälisches Institut für Wirtschaftsforschung, "Die wirtschaftliche Entwicklung in der Bundesrepublik Deutschland," *RWI-Konjunkturberichte*, vol. 42 (1991), pp. 69ff.

51. György Barabas and others, "Gesamtwirtschaftliche Effekte der Zuwanderung 1988 bis 1991," *RWI-Mitteilungen*, vol. 43 (1992), pp. 147ff.

52. For a critical discussion of 1990 and 1991 macroeconometric models of these effects, see Heilemann, "Economics of German Unification," p. 137. The interest rate on the rising deficits is still disputed. George Akerlof and others, "East Germany in from the Cold: The Economic Aftermath of Currency Union," *Brookings Papers on Economic Activity 1:1991*, pp. 39ff., seem to expect *no* effects on interest at all from German government deficits. McKibbin, "New Europe," pp. 16ff., expects deficits of the present magnitude to increase rates an average of 1.4 percentage points in Germany and 0.8 percentage point in the United States.

53. On this point, see Richard Freeman, "External Impacts and Adjustments to Government-Expenditure Shocks in a Dynamic Mode," discussion paper (Washington: Board of Governors of the Federal Reserve System, November 1991). Freeman correctly emphasizes a number of differences between the two situations but does not subscribe to the often heard German comment that the deficits reflect long-term investment in east Germany's production capacity.

54. Deutsche Bundesbank, *Report of the Deutsche Bundesbank for the Year 1991* (Frankfurt am Main, 1992), pp. 14ff.

55. Fritzsche and others, "Perspektiven," pp. 20ff.

56. In Bogai and others, "Arbeitsplatzförderung," pp. 12ff., or Priewe and Hickel, *Der Preis der Einheit*, pp. 121ff. Investment in production is reported to require DM 1,000 billion, housing DM 470 billion, environment DM 211 billion, energy sector DM 50 billion, transportation DM 210 billion, and telecommunications DM 60 billion.

57. Compare Lewis Alexander in "Comments and Discussion" to Rudiger Dornbusch, Federico Sturzenegger, and Holger Wolf, "Economic Transition in Eastern Germany," pp. 264ff., and Alexander, "Radical Reform in Germany," pp. 4ff., where the question of total factor productivity growth during the West German construction period is discussed: "For the years 1948 to 1951 total factor productivity is the most important factor contributing to growth; during later years the growth in total factor productivity falls back to more normal levels." For the general usefulness of the simple static allocation model, see Manfred Streit, "Einführung in die 2. Plenumsitzung der Jahrestagung 1991 des Vereins für Socialplitik," *Zeitschrift für Wirtschafts- und Sozialwissenschaften*, Beiheft 1 (1992), p. 53ff. For a comprehensive analysis of the *Wirtschaftswunder*, see also Rolf H. Dumke, "Reassessing the Wirtschaftswunder: Reconstruction and Postwar Growth in West Germany in an International Context," *Oxford Bulletin of Economics and Statistics*, vol. 52 (1990), pp. 451ff.

58. Immediately after unification the chemical industry was said to require a complete relocation because of heavy contamination. Now it is said that 85 percent of the total terrain has little or no need for cleanup. "Chemieindustrie registriert Aufbruch im Osten," *Süddeutsche Zeitung*, no. 152 (July 4–5, 1992), p. 21. An example from railways is often given as well, namely that doubling a one-way track requires at most twice the capital of a one-way track, though its capacity is five times greater.

59. The two strategies have been outlined in Sachverständigenrat, *Die wirtschaftliche Integration in Deutschland*, nos. 42ff. For a critical discussion, see Erhard Kantzenbach, "Thesen zur deutschen Wirtschaftspolitik," *Wirtschaftsdienst,* vol. 72 (1992), pp. 242ff.

60. Dornbusch and Wolf, *Economic Transition*, p. 240, table 2. The question of the proper exchange rate for deflation obscures any such determination, however.

61. Arbeitsgemeinschaft deutscher wirtschaftswissenschaftlicher Forschungsinstitute, *Frühjahrsprognose*, p. 32.

62. For a detailed analysis of bottlenecks in telecommunications, energy

and water supply, waste disposal, the education system, administrative capacities, and so forth, see Rüdiger Budde and others, *Übertragung regional-politischer Konzepte auf Ostdeutschland* (Essen: Untersuchungen des Rheinisch-Westfälischen Institutes für Wirtschaftsforschung, 1991), pp. 76ff.

63. The improvement of telecommunications is far ahead of schedule, and it will give east Germany the most advanced system in Europe. Wilhelm Pällmann, *Zehn Thesen zum Telekommunikations-Infrastrukturausbau in Ostdeutschland* (Berlin: Telekom, 1992).

64. The guiding principle for west Germany's regional policy has been to attract capital to labor and not the other way around.

65. Rheinisch-Westfälisches Institut für Wirtschaftsforschung, *RWI-Konjunkturbericht*, vol. 43 (1992), p. 57.

66. This number excluded people employed in the army, security organizations, and political parties, and those in vocational training. For 1992 the Institut für Arbeitsmarkt- und Berufsforschung expects a net 485,000 commuters to west Germany, half of whom will travel from more than 50 kilometers away. Bogai and others, "Arbeitsplatzförderung," p. 7.

67. Stolpe, *Schwieriger Aufbruch*, p. 56.

68. The administrative setbacks brought on by east Germany's adoption of the elaborate, rigid west German regulations were foreseen; even so, the GDR had very much insisted on adopting the FRG's legal framework at unification. Schäuble, *Der Vertrag*, p. 207.

69. Bernhard Lagemann, "Strukturwandel der Landwirtschaft in den neuen Bundesländern," *RWI-Mitteilungen*, vol. 43 (1992), pp. 61ff.

70. In 1989 the average annual income in East Germany was DM 10,000. In 1992 it will be about DM 14,500, compared to DM 26,500 in west Germany. In real terms the nominal increase of nearly 50 percent in east Germany will be about 20 percent. Rheinisch-Westfälisches Institut für Wirtschaftsforschung, *RWI-Konjunkturbericht*, p. 61.

71. WSI, press release, July 30, 1991, Düsseldorf.

72. Hans Dieter Hardes, "Lohnpolitische Konzeptionen für Ostdeutschland? Eine Analyse zu den lohntheoretischen Überlegungen des Sachverständigenrates," *Konjunkturpolitik*, vol. 37 (1991), pp. 156ff.

73. Institut für Wirtschaftsforschung, *Ostdeutschland*, pp. 90–91.

74. An often cited example is the bus driver who works in West Berlin, lives in East Berlin and hence is paid the east German wage tariff. In 1991 the income difference between unemployed and employed was DM 1,000 to DM 1,500, or about two-thirds, with the difference still on the rise. Institut für Wirtschaftsforschung, *Ostdeutschland*, pp. 43ff.

75. For the pros and cons of these suggestions see Akerlof and others, "East Germany in from the Cold," pp. 70ff. and pp. 87ff., and the large number of German papers it gave rise to—for instance, Frank Klanberg and Aloys Prinz, "Arbeitsmarktpolitik in den neuen Bundesländern: Mehr Irrwege als Auswege," *Wirtschaftsdienst*, vol. 71 (1991), pp. 397ff. Two recent discussions are Wolfgang Franz, "German Labour Markets after Unification" (Konstanz: Diskussionsbeiträge der Fakultät für Wirtschaftswissenschaften und Statistik

der Universität Konstanz, October 1991); and Lutz Bellmann, *Wage Policy in East Germany* (Nürnberg: Institut für Arbeitsmarkt- und Berufsforschung, 1991).

76. Fiscal costs may be even lower than calculated by Akerlof and others, "East Germany in from the Cold," pp. 71ff., if the subsidies' multiplier effects are taken into account. Interestingly enough, the great attention that Akerlof and colleagues attracted seems to be due to their fiscal prudence.

77. This holds at present for many of East Germany's exports to the former Soviet Union whose demand is price inelastic because of longstanding trade relations. East German employers see wage increases that are too rapid as a severe problem, but this is closely followed by the problems of financing investments, plants that are too old, local administration that is too slow, and marketing difficulties. See Deutsches Institut für Wirtschaftsforschung and Institut für Weltwirtschaft an der Universität Kiel, "Gesamtwirtschaftliche und unternehmerische Anpassungsprobleme in Ostdeutschland—Sechster Bericht," *DIW-Wochenbericht*, vol. 39 (1992), pp. 473ff.

78. Wage policy during the FRG reconstruction period was very much productivity oriented but also paid a high tribute to the still high unemployment. Ullrich Heilemann and Alexander Samarov, "Changes in the Determinants of the Rate of Change of Wage Rates in the FRG," *Jahrbücher für Nationalökonomie und Statistik*, vol. 205 (1990), pp. 452ff.

79. Charles P. Kindleberger, *Europe's Postwar Growth: The Role of Labour Supply* (Harvard University Press, 1967).

80. The subsidies may add up to a 100 percent depreciation of the investment in the first year, and the investment may be financed without any private means. "Zinssubventionen und sonstige Finanzierungshilfen im geeinten Deutschland," *Monatsberichte*, vol. 44 (August 1992), p. 28. For a detailed listing of the numerous subsidization programs, see Sachverständigenrat, *Die wirtschaftliche Integration in Deutschland*, p. 73, table 14.

81. These projections are based on the Chenery hypothesis. For the results of the estimates, their outside sample properties, and the additional assumptions made, see Roland Döhrn and Ullrich Heilemann, "Sectoral Change in Eastern Europe—The Chenery Hypothesis Reconsidered," in Leonhard Waverman and Bernhard Heitger, eds., *German Unification and the World Economy* (London: Routledge, forthcoming).

82. Rheinisch-Westfälisches Institut für Wirtschaftsforschung, *Konjunkturbericht*, pp. 48, 63.

83. Arbeitsgemeinschaft, *Frühjahrsdiagnose*, p. 15.

84. Housing investment, which is expected to increase significantly after 1993 when housing rents are freed, has been disappointing. This illustrates once again the conflict between consumption and investment in the short run. In the long run there will be harmful effects from postponing the decision to free rents.

West German foreign direct investment from 1984 to 1988 was only DM 12 billion annually. Furthermore, although the overall investment in east German manufacturing was only 0.9 percent of West Germany's investment, this share increased to 166 percent (if the companies owned by the Treuhand are left out). Institut für Wirtschaftsforschung, *Ostdeutschland*, p. 48.

85. Bogai and others, "Arbeitsplatzförderung," pp. 12ff.

86. Stolpe, *Schwieriger Aufbruch*, p. 76.

87. "Das EG-Werftenkonzept für Ostdeutschland," *Neue Zürcher Zeitung*, June 20, 1992, p. 16; "Subventionierte Projekte im Ost so überflüssig wie ein Kropf—Kriwet warnt vor unrentablen Investitionen," *Frankfurter Allgemeine Zeitung*, September 25, 1992, p. 20; and Institut für Wirtschaftsforschung, *Ostdeutschland*, p. 101. For the sectoral distribution of subsidies, see HWWA Institut für Wirtschaftsforschung, *Strukturbericht 1991*, pp. 256ff.

88. Christoph Schöffel, "Unternehmerische Engagements in den neuen Bundesländern. Eine Felduntersuchung," *iw-trends*, vol. 18 (1991), pp. 1ff.; and Institut für Wirtschaftsforschung, *Ostdeutschland*, pp. 56ff.

89. Gerhard Fels, Klaus-Werner Schatz, and Frank Wolter, "Der Zusammenhang zwischen Produktionsstruktur und Entwicklungsniveau," *Die Weltwirtschaft*, vol. 106 (1971), pp. 240ff.; and Döhrn and Heilemann, "Sectoral Change," p. 15.

90. Institut für Wirtschaftsforschung, *Ostdeutschland*, p. 55; and Robert Gerald Livingston, "United Germany: Bigger and Better," *Foreign Policy*, no. 87 (Summer 1992), p. 166.

91. Taking the average of the investment needs reported above (DM 1,500 billion to DM 2,000 billion over a twelve-year period), which comes to about DM 140 billion, disregarding that part that will be public investment, and assuming an east German support of DM 50 billion in savings for this purpose would imply DM 90 billion. For a scenario in which foreign capital would make up 50 percent of the total investments, see Jürgen Kröger and Manfred Teutemann, "The German Economy after Unification," EC economic papers 91 (Brussels: EC Commission, April 1992), pp. 29ff.

92. The relationship between national investment and saving or interest rates is still a puzzle. Although economic theory suggests there are no close links, empirical studies seem to find strong evidence for them. See Tamin Bayoumi, "Savings-Investment Correlations," IMF working paper 89/66 (Washington: International Monetary Fund, 1989), and the literature cited there. Unfortunately most of these studies suffer from the stylized character of the hypotheses tested. They often include only one explanatory variable, the factors influencing capital mobility are not explicitly tested, and there are considerable problems with the data base and the econometric methods employed. It is nevertheless interesting to note that Germany seems to have a strong and increasing investment-savings relationship. See Maurice Obstfeld, "How Integrated Are World Capital Markets? Some New Tests," NBER working paper 2075 (Cambridge, Mass.: National Bureau of Economic Research, 1986), table 6.

93. Institut für Wirtschaftsforschung, *Ostdeutschland*, p. 75.

94. The Ruhr area, the industrial heart of North Rhine–Westphalia, with a population of 5 million, had no university until well into the 1960s.

95. For parallels and differences between the conditions of the new Länder

and the older industrial regions see, for example, Rüdiger Hamm, "Umstrukturierungsprobleme in den neuen Bundesländern und Erfahrungsmuster altindustrieller Regionen," *Raumforschung und Raumordnung*, vol. 49 (1991), pp. 91ff.

96. Article 5 states that within two years of unification the legislative bodies of the united Germany should deal with the questions regarding amendments or additions to the Basic Law as raised in connection with German unification, particularly with regard to the relationship between the Federation and the Länder, and the possibility of restructuring the Berlin-Brandenburg area. Article 146 states that the Basic Law will lose its applicability when a new constitution has been approved by the German people and implemented.

97. Observers are very skeptical that a solution satisfying all parties can easily be found, given the great demands on the federal budget and the diverse, often opposing interests of the various Länder. Ralf Peffekoven, "Finanzausgleich im vereinten Deutschland," *Wirtschaftsdienst*, vol. 70 (1990), pp. 346ff.; Priewe and Hickel, *Der Preis der Einheit*, pp. 133ff.; and Wissenschaftlicher Beirat beim Bundesministerium der Finanzen, "Gutachten zum Länderfinanzausgleich" (Bonn, November 1992).

98. Abelshauser, "Entstehungsgeschichte der Sozialen Marktwirtschaft," pp. 19ff. In fact, a significant role for an economic expert advising in a critical situation seems to be the exception not the rule, and not only in Germany. See James A. Smith, *The Idea Brokers: Think Tanks and the Rise of the New Policy Elite* (Free Press, 1991), pp. 93ff. (the New Deal), and pp. 109ff. (Truman and the Council of Economic Advisers).

99. See Schäuble, *Der Vertrag*, pp. 209ff, p. 226.

100. See also Kreile, "Political Economy," pp. 68ff.; Priewe and Hickel, *Der Preis der Einheit*, pp. 189ff.; and P. J. J. Welfens, ed., *Economic Aspects of German Unification* (Berlin: Springer, 1992).

101. See Lutz Hoffmann, "Wider die ökonomische Vernunft," *Frankfurter Allgemeine Zeitung*, February 2, 1990, p. 15; and Kurt Nemitz, "Aktuelle Fragen der deutschen Währungspolitik," *Auszüge aus Presseartikeln*, no. 43 (1991), and the various references given there.

102. On the effects of increases in value-added and income taxes on selected households in east Germany and west Germany, see Fritzsche and others, *Perspektiven und Optionen*, pp. 29ff. In general, east German households would be affected only by increases in the VAT.

103. See Arbeitsgemeinschaft deutscher wirtschaftswissenschaftlicher Forschungsinstitute, *Die Lage der Weltwirtschaft und der deutschen Wirtschaft im Herbst (Frühjahr) 1990, [1991]* (Essen, 1990, 1991); Sachverständigenrat zur Begutachtung der gesamtwirtschaftlichen Entwicklung, *Auf dem Weg zur wirtschaftlichen Einheit* and *Die wirtschaftliche Integration in Deutschland*.

104. See Sachverständigenrat, *Auf dem Weg zur wirtschaftlichen Einheit*, p. 343. The basic idea of the export-base concept is that the economic and income base of a region may be built on activities that are independent of activities within the region, but are based on the region's exports.

105. See, for example, Budde and others, *Übertragung regionalpolitischer*

Konzepte, pp. 180ff. Under the present conditions the authors doubt the appropriateness of the FRG regional policy in east Germany with its stress on equalization and its weak emphasis on growth-oriented measures. They also point out statistical difficulties that this policy will create in the next few years. Given existing investment subsidies and future regulation of the federal fiscal equalization system, they recommend a more pragmatic regional policy for the near future, giving priority to improving the production-oriented infrastructure and removing bottlenecks.

106. Sachverständigenrat, *Die wirtschaftliche Integration in Deutschland*, p. 294; Priewe and Hickel, *Der Preis der Einheit*, pp. 178ff.; and Stolpe, *Schwieriger Aufbruch*, pp. 221ff.

107. Inotai, *Economic Impact of German Reunification*, p. 35.

108. For the missing theory see Helmstädter, "Neue Bundesländer als Industriestandort," pp. 96ff. For administration privileges see Lehmbruch, "Improvisierte Vereinigung," pp. 472ff.

109. In a letter to the Sachverständigenrat, the Wissenschaftliche Beiräte, and the five major German economic research institutes, Otto Schlecht, deputy minister of economics, asked for a halt to the discussion on the rationale behind economic unification and for a practical thinking on making unification a success (*Handelsblatt*, February 23–24, 1990). Among other things, he requested the economists to consider the conditions needed to make the transition without an exchange rate buffer.

110. Reinicke, *New Europe*, pp. 13ff., identifies the problem as holistic.

111. Most analyses of the current problems in Eastern Europe also deal with an only slightly modified stabilization context as encountered by the developed industrial countries or in the context of South American development (see Kornai, *Road to a Free Economy*, pp. 105ff., and the nine major tasks mentioned). Hardly a word is said about the vitalization of the East European economies. Except for stabilization models of the South American type, the frameworks and expertise of development economics seem to have hardly been applied, though development appears at first glance much more appropriate. Even if the analytical power of development economics is not overly impressive, it might be better to admit this and put what applies to use. A stimulating exposition of Eastern Europe's problems as those typical of developing countries is given by Ranis, *Global Perestroika*, p. 2; and Adam Przeworski, "The Neoliberal Fallacy," *Journal of Democracy*, vol. 3 (1992), pp. 45ff.

112. Wissenschaftlicher Beirat beim Bundesministerium für Wirtschaft, *Gesamtwirtschaftliche Orientierung bei drohender finanzieller Überforderung* (Bonn: Bundesministerium für Wirtschaft, July 12, 1992), pp. 13ff. In general, this report also concentrates on the phenomenological fiscal problems. The problems of labor and capital appear soluble only if the ground rules of economic activity are properly set, which the report finds is not yet the case.

113. Ernst Helmstädter, "Teutonomics II," *List Forum für Wirtschafts- und Finanzpolitik*, vol. 18 (1992), p. 6.